Public Parks, Private Partners

Central Park, New York City

Public Parks, Private Partners

———{ **How Partnerships Are Revitalizing Urban Parks** }———

Project for Public Spaces, Inc.

Kathy Madden
project director

Philip Myrick
project manager

Katherine Brower
researcher

Shirley Secunda
copy editor

Andrew Schwartz
editor

The Wallace-Reader's Digest Funds made this publication possible through its support of the Urban Parks Institute. Administered by Project for Public Spaces, Inc., the institute is part of the fund's Urban Parks Initiative that was launched in 1994 to increase the quality and accessibility of urban parks for public use, especially in underserved neighborhoods. The fund has committed $25 million over the past six years to help create, restore, or improve parks and greenways in cities across the country.

[Table of Contents]

I strongly believe that "town spirit," an old American phenomenon first identified by Alexis De Tocomenon, is reasserting itself. Municipal governments are becoming more creative and flexible of necessity, and this has made their attitude more welcoming to American citizens who are reasserting their fundamental right to create civic structures to administer certain civic needs. This synergy is making government in its turn more innovative, results-oriented, and accountable in the way in which it operates.

In 1831, de Tocqueville, a young Frenchman, arrived in America for the purpose of analyzing democracy as a system of governance. Because the young republic of the United States had embarked upon this novel experiment in human affairs with more direct intent than European nations where power still rested to a large degree in the hands of titular monarchs and a waning aristocracy, Tocqueville saw in this country the way of the future. How, he wondered, did a group of citizens organize themselves to accomplish the task of self-government? What useful lessons in political philosophy might he be able to share with his countrymen in a time of revolutionary change?

Tocqueville's book, Democracy in America has been published in several English language editions

Urban parks are especially good arenas for cooperation between municipal government and the citizenry.

and reprinted many times. In its pages many Americans have found, and continue to find, encouragement for their political initiatives as well as recognition of the presence of certain fundamental conditions that allow these initiatives to flourish.

"In America not only do municipal bodies exist, but they are kept alive and supported by town spirit," Toqueville wrote. Certainly these words are relevant to the work Project for Public Spaces has undertaken with the support of the Wallace-Reader's Digest Funds in providing assistance to civic organizations seeking to partner with municipal governments in the revitalization of urban parks.

Urban parks are especially good arenas for cooperation between municipal government and the citizenry. They are rife in opportunities for volunteerism. By analyzing the movement to create civic structures for park improvement and providing case studies that show what is being done all across the country, Project for Public Spaces is carrying forward what is perhaps the most important phenomenon and ideal that Tocqueville grasped and documented in Democracy in America: the essential vitality of local civic enterprise.

ELIZABETH BARLOW ROGERS
President of the Cityscape Institute, and former President of the Central Park Conservancy

I'm thrilled to see such a fabulous book outlining the importance of public-private partnerships in urban parks. Our restoration efforts here in Louisville would not have been possible without the dedication and hard work of our private partners. They have provided the political support, vision, and the private funding so critical to our success.

I believe public-private partnerships are a necessary part of successful park systems in the 21st century. The pressures on urban parks are as great today as they were in the days when Frederick Law Olmsted developed the nation's first generation of parks. The vision shown by our forefathers proved to be just that - a vision - of the vital role that public spaces play in the livability of our urban areas.

Our park systems across the country were important to the frivolity of the '20s, as spaces for cool breezes during the Depression, as victory gardens during WWII, and for our baby boomer families during the fifties. In the '60s and '70s they were the sites of demonstrations, lovefests and family outings. All too often, community parks have been the site of gang activities and drug deals in the '80s. The public-private partnerships

It is clear to me that leadership from both the public and private sector is necessary to provide the best parks for our citizens.

developed in the '90s proved to me that, with proper leadership and perseverance, we can restore those lands to places of beauty, community importance and neighborhood activities so important to revitalizing our cities.

This cannot be done successfully without regular community input into plans for future development of parks. The sense of ownership garnered by the community through involvement in planning is crucial to the long-term stewardship and enjoyment of these resources.

Leadership is the critical piece in all of the efforts to protect, restore or add to our urban parks systems. It is clear to me that leadership from both the public and private sector is necessary to provide the best parks for our citizens. That's why I am such an advocate of partnerships to keep our park systems intact or in making major additions to the system. Every child should have a park in his or her neighborhood that sparks imaginative play and appreciation for the natural environment. This book will be a great help to many citizens and officials who are dedicated to their parks.

MAYOR DAVID L. ARMSTRONG
City of Louisville, Kentucky

The rapid growth of the nonprofit sector in the United States during the last 20 years has had a particular impact on our country's public parks, as groups dedicated to the preservation and restoration of parks and open space are creating a buzz in cities across the land.

Urban leaders are asking if there are new or better parks partnership models for them to explore. Cities with small "friends of the parks" groups are looking to more substantive partnerships mainly to increase funding and maintenance for their parks, as well as community involvement in them. And cities with little or no nonprofit representation in their parks are seeking solutions to their budgetary and management shortfalls. As the rapidly expanding cities of the West develop new land for housing, environmental and recreation groups are advocating for new parks and greenways. In the North and Midwest, nonprofit groups are reclaiming formerly industrial areas for parks, re-using vacant lots for gardening, environmental education, and arts, and restoring grand old parks from the Olmsted era. And whether a group has been around for 30 years or 30 days, the chances are that its responsibilities are increasing.

All of this tells us that community groups that are organized and vocal can be important forces in establishing the priority for both recreation and open spaces in our cities. And these groups are helping cities transform parks into vital, active centers of urban neighborhoods and downtowns. As they become more involved, many of these groups are also willing to take on a certain amount of responsibility, even sharing the financial burden of maintaining their parks.

The specific reasons for establishing a nonprofit parks partnership are different from city to city. Often residents or local leaders from the private sector take the initiative to develop a relationship with the public sector to make park improvements because they have a vision for a better park and they acknowledge that the public sector may not be able to deliver the quality of service they desire. In other cases, a public agency has a vision or plan that goes beyond what it can achieve on its own without political, financial, or other assistance. Whatever the case, there are several compelling reasons for public/private partnerships[1] including:

Efficiency and Flexibility. A private group can act fast and save money—for example by purchasing park equipment or hiring repair crews on an as-needed or emergency basis. It also has the ability to be more flexible with staff and budget lines—being able to reconfigure them more easily in response to changing needs of the park. In addition, private groups are more open to experimenting with new or innovative park programs in an effort to be more responsive to park users.

Advocacy. A nonprofit may have the freedom and political will to speak out for budget increases, for increased security, or in favor of acquiring new parkland, while a parks department is constrained by and allied to the city's priorities.

Fundraising and Accepting Donations. Private donors often don't like to give to the public sector because they can't control how their money will be spent. In addition, there is often a distrust of giving money to any government bureaucracy, especially one that already has taxing power. Parks departments and other public entities with a public sector parks portfolio are, as a result, powerfully motivated to participate in or initiate a public/private partnership that can raise money. For their part, nonprofits often benefit from formal ties to a public agency, since it gives them added credentials to assure donors of long-term commitment and accountability to the public.

Focus: A nonprofit group that focuses specifically on one park may view that park, greenway, or other open space amenity more holistically than a parks department that has a responsibility to provide basic service to all the parks in a city or metropolitan area. While it is the usual practice of the parks department to treat a park as part of a larger open space system, a nonprofit may see it as part of a neighborhood—a perspective that can be reflected in its role in planning for park improvements. Additionally, public agencies often can't or don't want to manage small discreet projects, such as restorations of historic buildings, whereas private groups can devote the necessary attention to detail.

Community Ties: A private group often has better credibility with residents and local institutions than the local government does, allowing the nonprofit to facilitate meetings better, and tap key leaders for support and active engagement in the park.

Consistent Leadership: A mature nonprofit conservancy or friends group sometimes can provide more continuous leadership in a park or open space amenity than public officials can, as they are subject to politics and elections.

This book sets out to describe what roles these partnership organizations play in a park or greenway, what specific activities they perform and why they perform them, how they make agreements with their public sector partners, and the size and nature of their staffs, boards, and budgets.

In our research, we interviewed two dozen nonprofit park organizations and have attempted to provide a framework for how 16 of these organizations function as partners with public sector parks agencies. Throughout the document we have sprinkled the wisdom that the leaders of these organizations have provided us with, in an attempt both to share their knowledge and to suggest the powerful role that leadership plays in the process. Case studies of the organizations provide a more detailed view of their roles and structures, challenges, and issues with which they are engaged, and the parks, systems, and greenways around which they have formed. We hope they will serve as examples for practical application.

———[Part I]———

The Partnerships

—————[Chapter 1]—————

Why Build Partnerships for Parks?

In a city, a public space can be an asset or a liability. A main street or a park can be a symbol of a neighborhood's vitality and character, or an emblem of its disorganization and poverty of spirit. When it is an asset, it takes on the neighborhood's identity, becoming its star attraction and raising the quality of life, and property values, for residents.

In Brooklyn, New York, for example, Prospect Park functions as a sort of Main Street, as a different version of the idea of "downtown." It is a place where people come together, where they have a common investment that is both psychological and monetary, and where they locate the heart of their neighborhood. And many neighborhoods around the park, such as Park Slope and Prospect Park

South, bear the name proudly, as proximity to such a resource contributes substantially to their livability and economic value.

This is not always the case. Indeed many urban neighborhoods bear the names of their local parks like badges of shame. These parks are empty and underused, or spilling over with garbage and illicit activity. They are a liability for their neighborhoods. Of course, many cities and towns simply cannot allocate enough funds to their public spaces to maintain them and manage them at a reasonable level. The public pie has gotten smaller, and police, schools, and social services are considered higher priority areas. This can be partially attributed to several factors that have contributed to the rise of the nonprofit sector overall in this

The Long Meadow, Prospect Park.

Sailboat Pond, Central Park.

country, among them a shrinking tax base in cities in the northeastern United States, because of depopulation and massive federal cuts in urban programs that have forced cities to spend more money to achieve the same level of service to their citizens.

But money is not the only factor, for there are plenty of wealthy cities and towns that have empty main streets, barren parks, or parks that are simply a loose connection of ballfields and play areas. These spaces, instead of bringing people together, actually alienate them from one another. For those communities, parks are at best playgrounds, and at worst sad, humiliating places.

When people say that their neighborhood lacks a sense of community, this is what they mean. They feel that there is no way for them to participate in their public realm, whether as users, as volunteers, or as financial partners. Malls go up in the suburbs and a downtown deteriorates. A violent incident virtually eliminates use of a park. There may be hundreds of interested, caring individuals in the neighborhood who would like to volunteer, or contribute, or simply use that park or downtown in numbers, but they are not organized, and as a result nothing happens. As an incoming

parks director in Indianapolis in the early 1990s, Leon Younger discovered this phenomenon in regard to that city's inefficient, underused park system. "People wanted to help. I believe that people aspire to serve," said Younger. "However, we needed to create the mechanisms to allow them to invest in the park system."

In Indianapolis, those mechanisms took the form of community partnerships. In one case, the parks department gave maintenance responsibility for smaller parks to churches in the neighborhood, paying them a small fee to do it. This allowed Younger's park workers to concentrate on rebuilding the city's greenways and maintaining its flagship parks.

In New York City in the early 1970s, Elizabeth Barlow Rogers was running a summer youth program as part of the Parks Council volunteer association, a parks nonprofit advocacy group. Thinking about and working in Central Park caused her to notice this same phenomenon—a lack of mechanisms that allowed people to invest in the park. She wrote an article entitled "33 Ways Your Time and Money Can Help Save Central Park," which she described as "an L.L. Bean catalogue of opportunities." The next week, $25,000 in

$5, $25, and $50 contributions, flooded the Parks Council offices. "These checks," said Rogers, "were accompanied by wonderful memories. That's when I decided I had to stay and stick with the vision."[2]

Rogers eventually became the Central Park Administrator, a city position that was created specifically for her, as well as the president of the Central Park Conservancy, an organization she launched that now has raised over $110 million to restore the park and employs 216 in staff, including 172 positions in horticulture, maintenance, and programming. But New Yorkers don't judge the effectiveness of the conservancy by its funding and staff levels. They vote with their feet, visiting Central Park more than 16 million times every year.

Indeed "investment" is a word with many potential meanings. People invest in their parks with sweat equity—by clearing overgrown areas, maintaining gardens, and building paths, just as they contribute to the safety of their neighborhoods with watch programs. People invest with their savings, as they "adopt" trees or benches, allowing a cities and management organizations to take a longer-term perspective on maintenance and capital programs. And people invest in their parks as they use them, connecting their experiences with those of past generations and different cultures. They endow their parks with their cultural legacy.

Outreach, advocacy, marketing, promotion, programming, organizing volunteers-these are the ways to tap into the constituency of a public place. These kinds of activities, including outreach for capital campaigns and other fundraising efforts, convince people that somebody is doing something, and that the park has an advocate. More and more often, these efforts are an outgrowth of a public/private partnership. "The challenge," says Younger, "is to find people who have vision and who also know how to solve problems." Put another way, the important factors in making these mechanisms work are leadership and management, not money.

A Short History of Parks and the Role of Leadership

A typical history of urban parks in the United States begins in the 1850s, with William Cullen Bryant campaigning for, and Frederick Law Olmsted designing, Central Park in New York City. The notion of carving out a large space and designing it for recreation and enjoyment by everyone was a new concept, and required a tremendous amount of vision. Olmsted saw it as perfect expression of American Democracy. Although it was his first park commission, Olmsted knew what the stakes of his project were from the start. "It is of great importance as the first real park made in this country—a democratic development of the highest significance and on the success of which, in my opinion, much of the progress of art and aesthetic culture in this country is dependent."[3]

In Olmsted's parks, the wage earner as well as the patrician could use the park to its full advantage. These parks were indeed beautiful, and quickly begat expensive housing around them. As a result, the notion of large parks in urban settings caught on. Major cities such as Boston, San Francisco, Philadelphia, and Chicago, led the way with large parks of their own, and soon after, nearly every city wanted one.

As the country grappled with large-scale immigration at the turn of the 20th century, the notion of assimilation and the needs of newer Americans became an obvious focus of Progressive city government. As Galen Cranz has pointed out, this period, which she calls the Era of the Reform Park, was one of huge public investment, as parks were built on the sites of razed slums and programmed to solve the ills of the city instead of just provide an escape from them.[4] Much smaller parks were built, with field houses at their centers "the poor man's club house," Cranz calls it, and classes were held in English and civics, to help immigrants learn how to fill out tax forms and participate fully in the American democracy.

As the Reform Park movement scaled back during and after the Second World War, New York again set the example followed by many other American cities. Under the leadership of Parks

---

[2] Achieving Great Parks, Austin (Urban Parks Institute, 1996).

[3] Beveridge and Roucheleau, Frederick Law Olmsted: Designing the American Landscape, Rizzoli, New York, 1995.

[4] Cranz, Galen. The Politics of Park Design. MIT Press, 1982 see Chapter 2, p 61.

Commissioner Robert Moses, thousands of acres of parkland were bought and developed by the city. However, while parks gained large budgets and bureaucratic support, they lost their movement. Acquiring parkland became an end in and of itself, and cities built parkways along them and sports arenas inside them. Galen Cranz notes this shift in thinking about parks:

> Whereas earlier, park planners had to enumerate all the things that were being accomplished — reducing class conflict, socializing immigrants, stopping the spread of disease, educating people — to justify the unprecedented expenditure, under Moses parks had become a recognized governmental service needing no justification. The emphasis was instead on multiplying and extending into the suburbs and all the areas that didn't yet have a field house or some other kind of park. This is a sad period in a way, because it has very little artistic vision. And it has very little artistic vision because it has very little social vision. And this is why people sometimes think parks are boring.[5]

Somewhere between Olmsted and Moses, parks lost their critical urban function as places where people exercised their democratic muscles along with their biceps. They became merely recreational spaces, and as a result, when leadership disappeared, or budgets were squeezed, parks lost their funding. When the next sets of urban problems emerged, from drugs to depopulation, many cities pushed parks lower on the priorities list, instead of looking to parks for answers. As a result, parks were allowed to languish with outdated and under-funded maintenance and social programs. Crime-ridden, empty, and in various states of disrepair, they became part of the problem, instead of part of the solution.

The bureaucratization and re-prioritizing of parks departments had another effect-parks lost their cachet among the citizenry as well. Therefore, when Leon Younger arrived in Indianapolis in 1992, the parks department was one of the lowest ranking city departments in a newspaper poll. "Part of that decline was due to budget cuts," said Younger in a recent speech. "The parks department work force had shrunk from 800 employees to about 350 over ten years. However, in the process of cutting back park services, Indianapolis had lost its whole sense of the value that great parks can have for a city."[6]

What is needed to reverse this course of bureaucratic inertia and lack of vision is bold leadership, whether institutional or community based. Indeed, one cannot find a success story in the field where leadership, whether from the public or private sector, does not play a decisive role. In Denver, Colorado, a former state senator named Joe Shoemaker leveraged a $1.9 million investment into 150 miles of trails, boat launches, chutes, and parks in four counties and nine municipalities through and around the city in 20 years. A former parks director helped organize 12,000 volunteers in New Orleans who maintain and revitalize parks, trees, vacant lots, and the grassy medians of the city's famous boulevards. A park administrator in New York City "gives away" the park, section by section to community gardeners, teens, and volunteers, understanding that stewardship comes from earned authority.

The clear lesson from these successes is that with careful planning and genuine interest in residents and community issues, cities are discovering that their public parks are more than just expensive lawns to maintain. They are the seeding grounds for their neighborhoods and the places where people come together to help each other. With more citizen involvement in their design, maintenance, programming and use, city parks can achieve their true potential as the centers of their communities.

Indeed, one cannot find a success story in the field where leadership, whether from the public or private sector, does not play a decisive role.

[5] Cranz, "The Future of Parks" Parks as Community Places, 1997, Project For Public Spaces.

[6] Leon Younger, "Rebuilding the Indianapolis Parks System" p 32. Great Parks/Great Cities, A Leadership Forum, Project For Public Spaces, 1998.

Roles: How Nonprofits Work with Public Agencies

Nonprofit organizations can have a wide range of relationships and experiences with their public partners, depending upon the ability and resources of the city or municipality, and the condition of the park and its surrounding community. The nonprofits that we examined differ in age and stages of development. This provided us with an informative look at the kinds of issues faced by these organizations in creating and managing partnerships with the public sector over time. And while nonprofits are usually called "Friends of ... Park" or "The ... Park Conservancy" these names bear little relation to their actual role and do not necessarily indicate that they will be acting a particular way. Therefore, we have categorized these nonprofits according to the predominant role that they play in relation to the public sector.

Smaller nonprofits are typically **assistance providers**. These groups help parks departments with education, programming, and volunteers. They also advocate for increased funding for park improvements and expansion. These organizations primarily operate on a volunteer basis with few if any paid staff, and do not have any responsibility for the park itself.

New parks are sometimes initiated by nonprofits that act as **catalysts**. Such groups work with public agencies and others to initiate projects and provide financial support for new parks or greenways. These kinds of partners are typically involved in advocacy, design, and construction issues, and tend to be transitional in nature, redefining their role with the public entity and in relation to the park once the project is completed.

The groups attracting the most attention these days are the **co-managers**. Nonprofits of this type work in collaboration with the parks department by way of either: 1) a position jointly shared by the nonprofit and the parks department that oversees park planning, design and capital construction projects, and in some cases management and maintenance; or 2) a staff that works with the parks department and/or combines funds for the joint activities of master planning, capital project plans and construction. These groups share responsibility for the well-being of the park.

Some cities take the ultimate step of making a nonprofit the **sole managers** for a park. This kind of organization manages and maintains parks on its own, functioning as an independent entity with limited involvement of the parks department, and it shoulders the major responsibility for the park. In this structure, park policies tend to be determined by the nonprofit.

Finally, some groups are organized around an entire city or area park system, advocating for more city dollars and activity, training smaller friends groups, and initiating citywide greening programs. These **citywide partners** represent a different kind of park nonprofit, as they exist not to increase use and activity in a single park or greenway, but to raise the level and quality of open space and parks in an entire city, through neighborhood organizations and park partnerships.

Among our sample group, we found a few organizations that were involved in activities or had characteristics in common with more than one model. We also found that these types of working relationships tend to be fluid and dynamic, evolving as the nonprofit becomes part of the continuing effort to respond to the needs of the park over time. Thus, a newly-formed park nonprofit may start as an assistance provider and public advocate and, only after gaining experience and forming relationships with other organizations, later redefine or enlarge its role to work as a catalyst for the development of a new park or greenway project. Additional funding and staff, on the other hand, may draw a nonprofit into a more collaborative role with the parks department. A change in political situations can also affect a nonprofit's role, forcing the nonprofit into a leadership and advocacy position, or a re-examination of its current, active role in the face of a more progressive or activist government.

ASSISTANCE PROVIDERS

These groups that simply assist, support, or act as public advocates are a common type of partner relationship. Since volunteers who are not park professionals often staff them, these organizations usually act as public interest groups working on behalf of residents. Commonly referred to as "friends groups," these organizations-which may not be incorporated-typically have small operating budgets and do not have any responsibility for the park itself. They derive their power from their ability to rally a constituency for a park or potential open space, and in many cases, to raise outside funds.

While these groups are not seen as peers by their public sector partners, they do help parks departments considerably, providing additional labor, assisting in community outreach, and organizing park programs. They typically define their role as establishing public stewardship by organizing volunteers to assist in activities, such as cleanup days, and providing information to the public. Groups such as these may also involve themselves

Tree planting, Buttonwood Park.

heavily in fundraising, advocating for park improvements and expansion, public education, and programming. At times, such groups have been known to advocate for park issues and needs that they identify as not being addressed by the parks department.

In some cases, nonprofit organizations having this type of relationship with the public sector additionally get involved in facilitating community and political awareness meetings and workshops, as well as orchestrating new public and private sector partnerships to enable particular park projects to be realized. Examples of this nonprofit type are the Friends of Buttonwood Park, the Friends of Garfield Park, and the Great Plains Trail Network.

Assistance Provider Profile:
Friends of Buttonwood Park
New Bedford, Massachusetts

The Friends of Buttonwood Park was established in 1987 as a park advocacy and stewardship group to help implement a park master plan. Its staff is entirely volunteer, and the organization operates on an annual budget of approximately $3,500.

Some of the friends' activities have grown out of recommendations from the park master plan, including: providing and maintaining an outdoor reading space in conjunction with the public library; initiating a campaign to create and implement a pooper scooper law; and advocating for and instituting an end to the placement of memorial statues in the park through tree plantings with memorializing plaques. The Friends of Buttonwood Park was also active in molding a compromise to a $9 million zoo renovation in the park that impinged on the park's master plan.

The friends meet or talk informally with the parks department on a weekly basis to discuss issues. According to Jean Bennett, co-chair of the Friends of Buttonwood Park, "The friends have earned the respect of the parks department to the point where the administration would not do something in the park without apprising the friends of it."

A volunteer organization, the friends have a board comprised of 30 active members who work to promote stewardship, park programming, planting trees, and advocacy. The friends have hopes of expanding their working partnership with the city to become more directly responsible for managing and maintaining the park in the future.

CATALYSTS

Catalyst nonprofits are well known for their capacity to generate a vision, and initiate and facilitate a process that will bring that vision to the stage where it can be implemented. They can play a critical role in raising awareness, building community and political support, locating start-up funding, and orchestrating new partnerships among key players, such as parks departments, other government agencies, and private firms, to enable a park project to be realized from start to finish. Since they are organized to advocate for a park to be built, they tend to be transitional in nature, for once they complete their original mission, they must redefine their role in relation to the public sector and with the park project that they have seen to fruition.

Catalyst organizations such as these have been formed to create anything from regional greenway systems to small memorial groves within larger parks. In some cases, these organizations have been formed by citizens driven by a vision, while in other cases they have been formed by the public sector to help coordinate several entities, act as community liaisons, and raise funds. The National AIDS Memorial Grove and the Knox Greenways Coalition are examples of this type of group.

Catalyst Profile:
National AIDS Memorial Grove
San Francisco, California
The National AIDS Memorial Grove was established in 1989 by a small group of San Francisco residents who wanted to create a place for people to remember friends and loved ones who had died of AIDS. Now grown from a volunteer board to a paid staff of four, the organization is working with the San Francisco Recreation and Park Department to create the memorial out of a formerly neglected area of Golden Gate Park. The group has a 99-year lease on the grove site from the city, and it has replanted the area, installed memorial plaques and seating, and is in the process of fully endowing a full-time city gardener

Fern Grotto, National AIDS Memorial Grove.

position to maintain the grove over the period of the lease. As part of its mission, the group organizes monthly Saturday workdays where volunteers gather to weed, plant, and maintain the grove. The San Francisco Recreation and Parks Department is the primary park care provider and is responsible for security and maintenance.

Construction of the grove was near completion in spring, 2000 and the group was close to its endowment target. At this point, the board began to reexamine its focus. According to Thom Weyand, the grove's executive director, the board has broadened the organization's mission and envisions a shift from the creating and upkeep of the grove to that of "raising visibility for the grove as a national memorial and as a place for discussions about AIDS." The group will continue

TED WATHAN, QUADRANT

Bridle path, Iroquois Park, Louisville, Kentucky.

to be involved in civic beautification and urban reforestation activities and, since it must provide an annual grant to the city for the gardener and the ongoing maintenance of the site, it needs to have some type of oversight role into the future. As the organization's role in the grove project shifts direction, it may find itself redefining the working relationships it has with the San Francisco Recreation and Parks Department. It has even considered merging the operation with another national AIDS organization such as the NAMES project.

CO-MANAGERS

These nonprofits truly collaborate with their city partners by working together for the planning, design, and implementation of capital projects. They abide by policies set by their public sector co-managers and responsibilities for the park are shared. While all of these types of nonprofit organizations work closely with their partners, the roles and responsibilities of these collaborative partnerships differ, as do the ways in which the nonprofits are funded. The Central Park Conservancy, for example, is highly involved in maintenance, while the Louisville Olmsted Parks Conservancy is not.

Sometimes the collaborative working relationship is cemented by a joint position shared between the nonprofit and the parks department, simplifying the coordination of planning and staff resources. In some of these cases, the nonprofit organization and the parks department share the salary attached to the joint position. Organizations such as the Prospect Park Alliance, the Louisville Olmsted Parks Conservancy, and the Central Park Conservancy function along these lines.

Co-manager Profile 1:
Louisville Olmsted Parks Conservancy
Louisville, Kentucky
The Louisville Olmsted Parks Conservancy's involvement with the Louisville Park System (three major parks and the parkway system that connects them)

is structured so that the executive director of the Louisville Olmsted Parks Conservancy serves as the assistant director of the parks department, overseeing the planning and design division. The conservancy is housed in the parks department's offices, and parks staff works closely with conservancy staff in implementing park improvements. "The conservancy provides expertise in park planning and design, raises private funds to carry out programs and improvements, and creates community awareness in order to renew the parks and parkways as Frederick Law Olmsted might approach them today" says Karen High, landscape architect at the conservancy. The parks department does everything else, acting as contractor for the design and renovation work, and carrying out all maintenance and operations functions in the parks.

Co-manager Profile 2:
The Central Park Conservancy
New York, New York

The Central Park Conservancy's collaborative relationship with the city of New York and the Department of Parks and Recreation takes a very different approach from that of the Louisville Olmsted Parks Conservancy. Now primarily focused on managing, programming, and maintaining Central Park, the conservancy has a management contract that includes maintenance, public programming, and capital restoration.

A joint position between the partners has evolved over time as the roles and working relationships between the two organizations have changed. The first jointly held position was structured so that the parks department's Central Park administrator also served as the president of the conservancy. That made sense when, as in Louisville, the primary activity of the organization was rebuilding and renovating the park. Now that the park has undergone substantial renovation, though by no means complete, the conservancy has turned to maintenance, operations and programming as its core mission. Therefore, the structure of the partnership has evolved as well, and now the parks department's park administrator position is joined with the conservancy's senior vice-president for operations and capital projects. This joint position provides the authority to coordinate planning, capital development and park policy. The city retains poli-

cy responsibility for the park, ensuring that the park remains publicly accountable and continues to function consistently with other city parks.

A third type of co-manager partnership combines staff and/or construction funds without a formal organizational structure for joint activities such as master planning, capital project plans, and construction. This form of collaboration tends to be more project-focused, such as on developing or implementing a master plan, and implementing capital projects. Such nonprofits often raise and spend money for capital renovations themselves. Nonprofits such as the Piedmont Park Conservancy, Friends of Hermann Park, and Forest Park Forever follow this model.

SOLE MANAGERS

Although most cities retain control over the policy-making and maintenance functions of their public parks, a few give away nearly all the authority and responsibility to nonprofits. These almost fully autonomous organizations have the main responsibility for managing and maintaining individual parks and act with only limited involvement of parks departments. What really separates them from other organizations is that they are granted the power to develop and change policies related to the parks or greenways for which they are responsible. They are by definition heavily involved in maintenance and operations, and typically do much more than that. Examples of this type of nonprofit are the Yakima Greenway Foundation, and the Maymont Foundation.

Sole manager Profile:
The Maymont Foundation
Richmond, Virginia

The Maymont Foundation provides primary care for Maymont, a Victorian house and estate that is now a public park in Richmond, Virginia. While the foundation is responsible for virtually all aspects of the park, including fundraising and outreach, the issue of maintenance was foremost in its establishment in 1974. At that time, the foundation struck a deal with the city providing that it would maintain Maymont as a public park, if the city allowed it to manage and take over full

DARREN DESOI

The Maymont Estate

responsibility for this property. The foundation also receives an annual subsidy from the city for operating and managing costs.

The city is not involved in determining policy for the park as long as the foundation continues to keep the park open and free to visitors. The directors of the parks and recreation and the city planning departments sit on the foundation's board of directors together with a member of the city council. While the foundation has autonomy in most aspects of its role in the park, all major capital improvements must be approved by the city planning department. The foundation is not required to present the results of any master planning efforts to public bodies for approval.

CITYWIDE PARTNERS

Some groups are organized to focus on all or many parks and open spaces in a city, instead of on a single park. This role is fundamentally different from those outlined above. The main reason that these groups differ is that they bring existing expertise to neighborhoods and lend technical assistance in the formation and sustaining of new

parks organizations. There is no single model of a citywide partner organization. Some are closely linked with their parks departments; others operate outside the system completely.

Citywide Partner Profile:
Partnerships for Parks
New York, New York
Partnerships for Parks is a joint venture between New York City Parks and Recreation and the City Parks Foundation. It has two main functions-to cultivate grassroots and other organizations that are interested in taking care of parks, and to promote parks and green-friendly activities in the city. It considers the former to be its key role: to nurture friends groups through direct outreach and assistance, and to link them together into a strong, citywide constituency for parks and open space. To accomplish this, outreach coordinators in New York City's five boroughs provide links to the parks department for community and friends groups, who are given access to workshops and materials that Partnerships for Parks produces, everything from "How to Start a Friends Group" to "Tips on Planning Special Events." Certain parks and projects are given individual attention by a catalyst coordinator.

To fulfill its other role—to promote parks and park causes across the city—Partnerships for Parks coordinates citywide volunteer events, maintains a database of parks supporters, produces a newsletter, and advocates for parks issues. It is closely linked with the parks department-the two share offices and staff, and the nonprofit's $2 million operating budget is divided equally between the city and the private sector.

Activities: What Nonprofits Do For Parks

While every nonprofit provides its own unique type of support for a park, almost all nonprofit activities fall into the following nine categories:

1. Fundraising
2. Organizing volunteers
3. Design, planning and construction of capital improvements
4. Marketing and public outreach
5. Programming
6. Advocacy
7. Remedial maintenance
8. Routine maintenance
9. Security.

A nonprofit's activities are closely tied to its role in the park. For example, nearly all nonprofit organizations raise money. Most also organize volunteers and outreach efforts. Larger organizations may be involved in the design and execution of capital projects as well as regular maintenance of the park, and design professionals, as well as horticulturists and landscape historians, are key members of their staffs and boards. However, the more involved an organization becomes in the actual management of the park, the less likely it is to engage in outright advocacy. Therefore, many organizations stay out of more management oriented activities, such as routine maintenance, capital improvements, and security, not only because these options are more expensive and involved, but because they may compromise their ability to advocate. For example, if such groups are oriented to advocate for more public sector commitment to parks, they may feel strongly that the private sector has no place taking over management duties that the city should provide as a basic service. Of course, these groups may also engage in other activities such as marketing, outreach, and programming, or there may be another group in the city that performs some or all of those activities, along with advocacy.

1. FUNDRAISING

Fundraising is one of the most common activities that nonprofit organizations get involved in, not only because their tax-exempt status makes them eligible for funds from foundations and more attractive to individual donors, but also because it allows them to articulate concrete, visible park needs and goals. A nonprofit's ability to dedicate funds directly to a park project is particularly attractive to a city with a big vision but lack of funds to implement it. Fundraising also can serve as a park advocacy tool and raise awareness of the work of the nonprofit organization. It generally centers around three types of park needs: to supplement annual operating budgets, to implement capital projects, and to establish an endowment to ensure ongoing park maintenance, restoration, and management.

Fundraising for annual operating funds to supplement existing public operating budgets often involves membership drives and frequent low cost events, which have the added benefit of exposing infrequent or non-park users to the park and stimulating and encouraging longer-term involvement. Though donations are typically small, park outreach is great. Concession sales and educational programming fees are other sources for raising money that are often channeled into annual operating funds. Because they do not translate into visible projects in the park, and because some philanthropies will not give for this purpose, many nonprofits consider operating funds to be the most difficult kind of funds to raise.

Fundraising for capital campaigns tends to rely more on personal solicitations to individual and corporate donors than on events. Once the capital money is raised, design and construction is often carried out by the parks department or contracted out to private firms. Fundraising for endowment campaigns, like capital campaigns, tends to focus on larger donations from private individuals and corporations as well as matching grants from foundations. Of course, public partners can provide fundraising help as well, acting as agents to receive federal, state, and local grants and opportunities, and pursuing grants from government sources.

Fundraising Profile: Forest Park Forever
St. Louis, Missouri

Since it was established in 1986, Forest Park Forever has been heavily involved in fundraising activities. The group runs three different fundraising efforts: an annual "Friends" membership campaign; "Restoring the Glory," a mammoth $43 million capital restoration campaign that is being conducted to match funds pledged by the city of St. Louis; and a Forest Park Trust to establish an endowment for ongoing park maintenance. According to Jim Mann, Forest Park Forever's executive director, the three campaigns target different audiences and require different types of fundraising activities and events.

The annual "Friends" campaign combines a membership drive with a drive to raise funds for annual operating expenses and park maintenance. Individuals, foundations, and corporations are asked to join and contribute to reach the $2.5 million per year goal. "The fundraising events are inexpensive and are aimed toward encouraging park usage," says Mann. One particularly successful event is the annual "Directors Tour," where members who have contributed $150 or more are invited for a bus tour of the park given by the executive director. Light refreshments are served, and brochures about the park, including self-guided walking tours, are handed to participants as they step off the bus. Other events encourage park usage for members, such as special invitations to visit the Forest Park Forever booth at the park's annual Kite Festival and Hot Air Balloon Race. Some of these special invitations are combined with a raffle for a roundtrip flight donated by an airline to a destination of choice.

FOREST PARK FOREVER

Forest Park, St. Louis, Missouri

Fundraising efforts for the "Restoring the Glory" capital campaign are part of a joint effort between the city and Forest Park Forever to each raise $43 million dollars for "improvements to the infrastructure, environment, athletic facilities and buildings in the park." For this effort, Forest Park Forever focuses on larger donors and corporations.

One particularly successful program is Forest Park Forever's Progress Plus program, which uses tax credits and matching grants to leverage donations up to five times the cost of a corporation's actual contribution. The first incentive for corporate gifts is the ability to earn a 50 percent state tax credit. A second incentive, a challenge grant from the Danforth Foundation, designed to expand corporate philanthropy beyond the usual donors, stretches the corporation's gift with an additional $0.50 for every dollar contributed. For example, a contribution of $250,000, which costs a corporation $71,000 after tax deductions, can equal $375,000 for the park.

In order to qualify for the maximum Danforth Foundation contribution of $5 million, Forest Park Forever must raise $10 million from corporations that are not part of the elite 30 "Civic Progress" member companies. One fundraising effort as part of this campaign has entailed asking six corporations to invite 20 companies each to attend a cocktail party that featured a discussion of park restoration efforts. Two of these events have been held so far. At one of these events, a company donated the use of their helicopter for those interested in experiencing a bird's eye view of the park. By July 1999, Forest Park Forever had raised more than $37 million towards their total $43 million goal, and $8 million toward Progress Plus.

A new effort, the Forest Park Trust campaign, seeks to raise $5 million to establish an endowment for ongoing park maintenance. Relying on solicited donations from private individuals, corporations and foundations, the campaign has already raised over half of its goal. While the push to date has been on the annual and capital campaigns, it is thought that some of these annual funds will be added to the endowment in the future.

Fundraising that has an outreach component is also important. The "Pennies for the Park" campaign, which began with the idea of putting donation cans in schools and stores in the metro area, has taken off. Incredibly, St. Louis' major downtown mall, The Galleria, has promised to match the donations in the campaign with $50,000 of its own money. 50 stores in the mall are participating in the campaign, and the mall's giant fountain generates $8,000 for the park in what is perhaps the most effortless fundraising event imaginable. "More important than the money is the visibility," says Lee Anna Good, Forest Park Forever's marketing and capital campaign director, who adds that the pennies campaign builds the organization's identity and helps encourage the public to think of the park as an institution in and of itself.

> *Fundraising that has an outreach component is also important.*

2. ORGANIZING VOLUNTEERS

Volunteers play an important role for all nonprofit organizations, often significantly building community stewardship, support, and involvement with the park. Nonprofits often organize volunteers to participate in remedial maintenance activities such as weed removal, trail and path upkeep, and park clean-up days. Volunteers also commonly help organize and staff public park events, produce and send newsletters and other organizational mailings, and solicit park donations. They can be valuable assets to the park as trained docents, providers of visitor information, education and outreach, and park security, as well as collectors of park usership information.

Organizing Volunteers Profile:
The Great Plains Trail Network
Lincoln, Nebraska
Volunteers are the mainstay of the Great Plains Trail Network (GPTN), an all-volunteer organization focused on advocacy and fundraising for the acquisition and development of the Lincoln Area Trails Network in and around Lincoln, Nebraska.

ELAINE HAMMER, GPTN

Volunteers deck the Highland Bridge on the Mopac East Trail in Lincoln, Nebraska.

According to V.T. Miller, membership coordinator for the organization, the GPTN solicits volunteers during annual membership drives. On the same form as membership registration and renewal, members are asked to check off the types of activities in which they are interested in participating: speaking to groups, mailings, fundraising, or helping with events. A database of all volunteers and their areas of interest is maintained and drawn upon to organize various activities.

One of the most interesting ways that nonprofits use volunteers is in gathering information about the parks or trail network. GPTN organizes volunteers annually to conduct a census of the trails at 8 to 10 different locations. GPTN not only uses the information to publicize the trail to the newspapers, but the Parks and Recreation Department, which owns and maintains the trails, makes of use the information for allocating budget resources and to find out about safety issues. Issues of safety are determined based upon information about level of trail usage, the times of day trails are most used, and the numbers of bicyclists and skaters who wear helmets.

3. DESIGN, PLANNING, AND CONSTRUCTION OF CAPITAL PROJECTS.

Often a park has a conservancy or friends group attached to it because the park is suffering from neglect and needs to be substantially repaired. It is the role of many of our featured organizations to raise funds and organize volunteers to restore such parks, and capital projects are the main vehicle for those restoration efforts. As a result, nonprofits can get involved in any number of activities related to capital projects: from reviewing projects proposed and developed by the parks department, to contracting out design and implementation, or even to actual in-house design and construction of particular projects.

Most of the nonprofits we surveyed leave the construction of large projects to the public sector, which is usually more capable with costly projects that could overwhelm a private group (the Maymont Park Foundation and Central Park Conservancy being notable exceptions). However, some groups will manage projects every step of the way. Developing an overall vision for the park through a master plan is still another form of planning for capital projects. Whatever the case, most capital planning requires strong leadership and an effective working partnership to negotiate its inevitable complexities and elaborate decision-making process (although even a fledgling nonprofit can have a dramatic influence by virtue of its fundraising efforts and community credibility). Just over half of the organizations we reviewed were involved in capital planning.

In addition, nonprofits can make innovation in design a priority. Many parks departments, both to cut costs and to streamline operations, accept what are known as "cookie cutter" designs, that is, the same design over and over for different facilities. Many of the nonprofits that we are familiar with have inspired radically new design ideas, or prompted designs that are contextually fitting with a surrounding historical landscape, both by working closely with new designers, by emphasizing the ideas of residents, and by attempting to make each design specific to individual parts of the park that are being addressed.

Capital Projects Profile:
Louisville Olmsted Parks Conservancy
Louisville, Kentucky
The Louisville Olmsted Parks Conservancy was formed to take on the restoration and revitalization of Louisville 's Olmsted parks, and it continues to function as a project-oriented design and planning team that focuses on the system's historic value. According to Susan Rademacher, executive director of the conservancy, "there had been a complete loss of institutional memory [in the parks department] about what these Olmsted landscapes were designed to do, how to manage them, and how to provide programs that would encourage public use." On an almost daily basis, the conservancy staff rolls up its sleeves over plans that it develops jointly with the design staff of the parks department, which houses the conservancy's offices. The conservancy's scope of work includes implementing the master plan with phased capital projects, design, overseeing and reviewing projects in all of Louisville's Olmsted parks, landscaping and restoration (often using volunteers), raising private capital dollars to supplement public

money, and creating programs to attract new users.

Parks department staff usually get involved in design and project management, working under the assistant parks director, who is also the executive director of the conservancy, This interlocking relationship is enhanced by a system of checks and balances: the conservancy reviews all projects and can reject them if they don't conform to the master plan; meanwhile the parks department must approve all conservancy capital projects and programs.

One of the partnership's first projects together was the creation of a multi-use trail in Cherokee Park that would require four bridges, restoration of woodlands, and a sensitive design to fit it within the historical landscape. The "pre-planning" phase involved a team made up of the conservancy, parks department staff from the design, engineering and maintenance departments, as well as outside consultants in landscape architecture, ecology, engineering and historic landscapes. In an all-day meeting that included site visits, this team identified key issues and drew up a scope of work that could be bid on by sub-consultants. In the next phase, consultants presented their drawings and ideas, which the parks department and conservancy's construction committee reviewed together on a monthly basis. According to Michael Smiley, the project manager working for the parks department at the time, the department focused primarily on the maintenance and management impacts of the design, while conservancy staff concentrated more on ensuring that the design was of the highest quality, met historical and ecological objectives, and followed the master plan. Finally, a team of parks department engineers, designers and conservancy staff and board members jointly reviewed the final construction drawings presented by the consultant. Smiley explained that this collaborative team worked together almost as if it were its own organization, spending countless hours marking up plans and monitoring construction on-site to ensure that the contractors were meeting the highest construction standards. This project required extensive use of consultants in the pre-planning since it was among the first projects undertaken by the partnership upon completion of the master plan. Much of that outside expertise now has been absorbed by the staffs of the conservancy and the parks department, who now understand much more about how to design within the historic context of the Olmsted landscapes.

Since city funding is limited, the parks department funds basics like infrastructure and operations; the conservancy focuses on improving the park experience, providing a greater variety of recreation and landscapes, improving character, and doing experimental projects such as wetlands restoration.

4. OUTREACH AND MARKETING

A nonprofit has an obvious rationale for engaging in outreach and marketing. These activities can build usership, educate users, encourage stewardship, and create support—whether financial, volunteer or political—for the park and for park issues. This is also a common way to enhance the image and credibility of the park organization in the community. Marketing also can be used to create new relationships with other institutions through joint publicity and programming as well as promoting and increasing public involvement in park issues and development. Typical mechanisms include: direct mail and newsletters; press coverage; greeter programs; high-visibility events that help bring attention to specific park needs; and meetings with local community groups or institutions such as schools and faith-based organizations.

Outreach and Marketing Profile:
Prospect Park Alliance
Brooklyn, New York
Since 1980, when the Prospect Park Administrator's Office was created, usership in Prospect Park has grown from 1.7 million people per year to over 6 million in 1998. Tupper Thomas, the park's administrator and the president of the nonprofit Prospect Park Alliance, gives much of the credit for that shift to an approach that includes local residents in many aspects of park management, including identifying and prioritizing improvements and incubating new programs.

The alliance's strategies for increasing awareness about the park include: cross marketing with nearby institutions (the Brooklyn Public Library, Brooklyn Museum of Art, and Brooklyn Botanic Garden) to create a multipurpose destination;

public information (newsletters, greeter programs, the press and direct mail); interviews with local leaders and presentations to community associations; and programs and special events that highlight the culture of specific populations.

However, the alliance's grassroots community outreach is what distinguishes it the most from other organizations. To strengthen connections with nearby neighborhoods, whose diverse populations were previously under-represented in park decision-making, a cultural anthropologist and alliance staff interviewed local leaders from different ethnic groups that were located through churches, health care centers, and educational institutions. The information helped the alliance understand cultural considerations that might open new opportunities to provide a park experience that was more relevant to these groups.

The interviews also introduced the alliance to many new community groups who were then asked to serve on a Community Committee, formed in 1997 to help develop new programs, prioritize capital improvements, and build awareness about the park. The Prospect Park Community Committee now represents more than 60 neighborhood cultural and political associations in Brooklyn. The committee is working to develop a Comprehensive Plan for the park, which will serve as the guiding document in the alliance's development over the next 10 years. According to Thomas, there are other benefits as well. "When people come to the meetings, they exchange a wealth of ideas about their neighborhoods in addition to ideas about Prospect Park. It is as if parks are a safe place politically, a place where people can talk about lots of other issues. The Community Committee also very effectively talks to our elected officials about the importance of funding for all the parks in Brooklyn," she said.

Cultural programs and events also have raised the profile of the park, especially among ethnic populations that are ever more prevalent in Brooklyn, but don't necessarily frequent the park. For example, the Haitian festival drew over 2,000 members of the Haitian community to the park and brought in new Haitian volunteers and many new contacts for the Community Committee.

Park user groups are also an important constituency with which the alliance works, often to

Cultural programs and events serve the extremely diverse communities that surround Prospect Park.

the benefit of everyone involved. For example, the alliance helped organize the park's dog walkers, who then established FIDO (Fellowship in the Interests of Dogs and their Owners), a group that now monitors all dogs in the park and makes sure they follow leash laws, but also ensures that dog issues receive fair consideration.

5. PROGRAMMING

Programming can be the key difference between a well-used park and an empty one, regardless of financial support. It is also an area where the flexibility of a nonprofit can be particularly useful-some city parks departments find it hard to change programs that have been in place for long periods of time but get little use. While occasionally a nonprofit will manage recreation programs-typically thought of as being the province of the city-more often the partnership will engage in activities that compliment and enhance the programs already provided by the city.

Nonprofit programming activities are often broad in scope, focusing on environmental issues and education, theater and arts festivals, recreation, after school programs, and summer day camps, to name just a few. Programs are aimed at a variety of audience ages, cultural backgrounds, and neighborhoods across the city, though youth are usually the main target. Typical programs aim toward building community stewardship, cultural and environmental awareness, interpersonal skills and team building, teach new skills, and introduce and attract visitors to underutilized areas of the park, among many other activities.

Programming Profile:
Friends of Hermann Park
Houston, Texas

Hermann Park in Houston, Texas is currently undergoing a dramatic transformation guided by the Friends of Hermann Park. As a key part of that transformation, the friends are redeveloping the Bayou Parkland, a riparian and woodland environment comprising a quarter of Hermann Park's 400 acres. However, demonstrating the Bayou Parkland's relevance to residents is complicated, in part because six-lane MacGregor Drive and a large hospital on the southwest boundary block access to and prevent parking near this interior park area. In an earlier planning study conducted by the friends, it was revealed that many residents were unaware that the Bayou Parkland is part of Hermann Park at all.

The friends understood that in order to attract

users to this difficult but potential-laden site, they would first need to do two things: make structural improvements, and introduce people to the place by actually bringing them to it through programming.

Because of its mix of woodland and wetland areas, the Bayou Parkland was an obvious place for the friends to lead environmental programs. They decided on a targeted approach that basically test marketed programming elements with a group of children from seven local elementary schools. This pilot project, known as After School Adventures, was a science enhancement program for these nearby schools. Once a week, staff from Friends of Herman Park would go to a school and lead activities and field trips for students registered in the program. 406 students from the seven different schools and a women's shelter participated during the year and-a-half this program was in operation.

By watching the students go through the environmental program and then extensively surveying them, their teachers, and their parents afterward for suggestions and recommendations for improvements, the staff was able to quickly work the kinks out of the program, and come up with a series of changes to the site, including amenities, signage, and trail improvements. Experience with teachers' requirements, students' needs, curricula develop-

ment, and transportation logistics led almost immediately to the formation of a much larger and broader program, "Field Studies 101," that added a key element - it trained the teachers to run the program themselves. During six weeks in the fall of 1997, 2,656 budding naturalists and their teachers participated in Field Studies 101. Importantly, the friends' evaluations have contributed directly to their ability to continue to expand the program, and raise awareness among interested users, donors, and others for the capital improvements necessary to bring in other groups, and for different activities, both active and passive.

6. ADVOCACY

Some of the organizations we studied sprang from older, advocacy-focused "friends" groups, and were established specifically to be more moderate, project-focused organizations that could partner with the city on capital improvements. In some cases it was the reverse—an existing conservancy helped birth a separate, independent group that would be an advocate. If the rule is that a partner must not poison the well by criticizing another partner, that still leaves room for the nonprofit to promote more action

Youth participate in an environmental education program conducted by the Friends of Hermann Park.

FRIENDS OF HERMANN PARK

from other city agencies (such as more police presence or road improvements) and more funding from the city or state. In fact, effective advocacy campaigns—often waged in local newspapers and through media events—can help legitimize both the nonprofit and the parks department in the eyes of the general public and potential funders.

Advocacy incorporates a wide range of activities, such as putting pressure on the city for increased park funding, expanding or developing new parks or greenways, preserving historical design, improving basic maintenance, and increasing playground and general park safety. Typically, as a nonprofit increases its involvement in management, it reduces its role as public advocate. Thus, many groups that share responsibilities for the park with the public sector are less involved in overt advocacy activities, finding it complicates their working relationship. They may, however, be substantially involved in advocating for parks issues behind the scenes, especially if they are successful groups and have gained political influence as a result. On the other hand, many groups with smaller operational budgets find advocacy and lobbying activities more conducive to their roles as assistance providers, because it helps them spearhead new visions and facilitate change.

Effective advocacy campaigns can help legitimize both the nonprofit and the parks department.

A further tool used by some unincorporated groups to facilitate their advocacy activities is to partner with another nonprofit organization with 501(c)(3) status in order to receive tax-deductible contributions for park and trail acquisition and development. In this way, a group can raise funds, but preserves its right to actively lobby political bodies on park and trail issues and the ability to involve itself in political campaigning and support. For example, the Great Plains Trail Network has purposefully avoided obtaining 501(c)(3) status and has no formal affiliations with other park, civic groups or institutions so that it can preserve its right to actively lobby political bodies on trail issues and on behalf of trail supportive political candidates. In order to facilitate its fundraising activities, the board has arranged with the Nebraska Trails Foundation to receive contributions for trail acquisition and development. However, this practice is not without controversy, and the board is considering establishing a foundation to raise money for trail maintenance activities in the future.

Advocacy Profile:

The Knox Greenways Coalition

Knoxville, Tennessee

Established in 1992 by six conservationists, the Knox Greenways Coalition, a nonprofit grassroots citizens group, was formed to advocate for and help develop a greenway and trail system within the city and county of Knoxville. Over a period of five years, the coalition has successfully created partnerships with the city and county and integrated the idea of a large-scale greenway system into public plans and projects. Having facilitated the creation of city and county greenway coordinator positions, subsequently staffed by two founding members of the coalition, and a Mayor's Greenway Advisory Committee, the vision and plan for the greenway is now in place. With 12.8 miles built to date and 200-300 miles in different stages of planning and design, the coalition has redirected its mission to sustain pressure for continued development of the greenway. The coalition lobbies for financial and political support through its presence and active involvement in the Mayor's Greenways Advisory Committee, by representing the greenway at meetings on city issues, and through organizing planning, community, and political activities focusing on the greenway. Coalition volunteers meet with community and neighborhood groups interested in developing a portion of the greenway in their areas and help them to organize and develop actual designs. The coalition also holds a five-kilometer run fundraiser and an annual awards ceremony for elected officials, neighborhood organizers, and for people who have helped facilitate the trail through the giving of easements and/or an involvement in trail maintenance.

CITY OF KNOXVILLE

Jean Teague Greenway, Knoxville, Tennessee.

7. REMEDIAL MAINTENANCE

Many parks require a high level of maintenance, and city parks departments are typically limited in their ability to provide what is required, above a minimum standard. Therefore, parks nonprofits of all sizes organize maintenance volunteers or contract out maintenance tasks that seem to be beyond the capacity or budget of the primary caretaker. Typically, remedial maintenance work is done in response to a chronic, but critical need such as replanting, path repair, weeding, and erosion control. A seasonal "clean-up" day with volunteers is also a typical remedial maintenance function. Reclaiming neglected areas of the park, through community gardening or replanting, as well as repairs after storms or floods, are not beyond the scope or ability of volunteers.

Just under one third of the nonprofit organizations we reviewed are involved in remedial maintenance. All but one of these organizations was involved in routine maintenance as well. This suggests that involvement in one is easily combined with the other. The organizations from our sample group that perform remedial maintenance tasks are: The Central Park Conservancy, the Maymont Foundation, the Yakima Greenway Foundation, the Piedmont Park Conservancy, the National AIDS Memorial Grove, Friends of Buttonwood Park, and the Knox Greenways Coalition.

Remedial Maintenance Profile:
Yakima Greenway Foundation
Yakima County, Washington

The Yakima Greenway Foundation is responsible for all activities and maintenance related to the Yakima Greenway in Yakima County, Washington. The city and county do not monetarily contribute to the greenway at all. Through a partnership with the American Association of Retired Persons, who pay seniors to do small tasks for supplementary income, the Yakima Greenway Foundation gets supplemental help painting, cleaning and weeding along the greenway. In addition, the foundation uses every possible volunteer group to help out with maintenance, including the Eagle Scouts, who earn merit badges for routine maintenance tasks, like painting picnic tables and benches, and repairing flood damage. Even county work crews from local prisons are brought in to pick up trash along the greenway.

8. ROUTINE MAINTENANCE

Many nonprofits decide to leave routine maintenance to the public sector, taking on responsibilities for other activities that will free up parks departments to better accomplish the task. Only about a third of the groups we studied currently do routine maintenance, other groups being loath to give the public sector an opportunity to relinquish their traditional responsibility for basic service and, at the same time, not having the staff and equipment to carry the responsibility.

On the other hand, routine maintenance is often where public funding shortfalls are most obvious. While most nonprofits choose not to tackle this activity at the start, many state that they will at least consider taking it on sometime in the future. Reasons for this change down the road include the desire for more autonomy, the ability to more quickly respond to this need, and better overall coordination if one entity is responsible for management of the whole park.

Routine maintenance activities include day-to-day tree and lawn care, litter removal, small repairs and painting. While many routine maintenance activities are well within the capability of a friends group and trained volunteers, it is still most com-

YAKIMA GREENWAY FOUNDATION

Volunteers help plant a new flower bed in Sarg Hubbard Park on the Yakima Greenway.

mon for nonprofit involvement in routine maintenance to be supplemental to what is primarily the
parks department's responsibility. Examples of
nonprofit park groups that actually take primary
responsibility for routine maintenance are the
Central Park Conservancy and the Maymont
Foundation — well-funded and staffed partners
that have negotiated considerable control over all
aspects of their parks. Other examples exist in new
development projects, especially greenway efforts
led by nonprofits, such as the Yakima Greenway
Foundation, who make new projects more attractive to the public agency by committing to do the
maintenance, thereby reducing the potential additional burden on the parks department.

Routine Maintenance Profile:
The Central Park Conservancy
New York, New York
Although it has been in existence since 1980, a
change in the Central Park Conservancy's management style in 1994 has helped to make dramatic
improvements in the overall maintenance of
Central Park. A new zone-based system replaced a
decades-old tradition of maintenance crews that
worked all over the park as a team — an approach
that discouraged accountability since work not
done could not be traced to a single person in
charge. Now, each of 49 zones, roughly 10 acres
each, are the direct responsibility of a zone gardener whose task is not only to maintain horticultural

standards, but also to remove minor graffiti, empty trash baskets, do small-scale mowing, repair benches, and address potential crime situations. "When we went from a crew-based management structure to a zone-based structure, we immediately saw significant improvements in cleanliness and horticultural care throughout the park," said Doug Blonsky, the current administrator for Central Park.

"Zone-based management calls for direct accountability by an individual for his or her zone and instills a sense of pride and ownership," adds Blonsky. "Providing a uniformed presence, zone gardeners become familiar to regular park patrons and often develop relationships with them. The zone gardeners are the core of our maintenance philosophy in Central Park."

Zone gardeners are not on their own - each gardener has his or her own crew, and receives assistance from specialty crews. "Park-wide specialty crews are still essential to support the zone gardeners in such areas as graffiti removal, bench repair, tree care, and turf care," says Blonsky. Although these support crews specialize in a particular maintenance area such as clearing storm sewers and drains, repairing bridges and historic structures, etc., they also help with general repairs and restoration wherever needed. Each zone gardener also manages a regular team of volunteers.

The Central Park Conservancy has a budget of approximately $7 million for horticulture, maintenance and operations. Altogether, 150 maintenance staffers take care of the park—a mix of city and conservancy employees all of whom report to the administrator.

9. SECURITY

Although safety is typically a critical need in many neglected or underused urban parks, few of the nonprofit organizations we reviewed included security as a primary activity. There are some obvious explanations for this discrepancy — lack of

Simply by working on their main mission— encouraging use of a public park, all groups are involved in promoting security.

involvement by nonprofits in security issues may be because of an inability to afford staff costs, a lack of technical training, or, more likely, a reluctance of the organization to become associated or involved with regulatory, policing or enforcement issues.

However, we would like to think that many groups did not identify security as a primary activity for their organization because, as we stated in Chapter 1, the relative safety of a public park is more dependent on its use than on any other single factor. Therefore, "security" measures such as hiring rangers to patrol an area, can contribute to an overall strategy for bringing people back into a park but it is a small part of the security equation. Access, visibility, appearance, and use are all more important factors. Simply by working on their main mission—encouraging use of a public park, all groups are involved in promoting security.

However, some nonprofit park management organizations do provide a measure of official "security" for park users. These activities may take the form of volunteer rangers—who function very much like a neighborhood watch patrol—or professional security staff, responsible for policing the grounds and enforcing regulations themselves. Although only two of the organizations we interviewed are currently involved in security provision as a primary part of their orga-

PROJECT FOR PUBLIC SPACES

The Central Park Conservancy completed renovations on the park's 5-acre Great Lawn in 1997, at a cost of $18.2 million.

nizational activities, a few additional organizations in our case study pool indicated that they expected to increase their involvement in park security within the next five years.

Security Profile:
Piedmont Park Conservancy
Atlanta, Georgia

In 1998, the Piedmont Park Conservancy conducted a market survey[7] that revealed that safety in the park was a big concern among the public. To address the issue, the conservancy initiated the "Ambassador Program," which, in its first year, trained four part-time seasonal staff to greet visitors and report incidents, via walkie-talkie, to a city-contracted park security guard who had been employed for years to monitor illegal parking, but was unable to address other problems since he was tied to his guard post. The conservancy feels the program has contributed enormously to the public's perception of safety, since ambassadors are a more mobile and visible patrol.

The ambassador program was modeled on the Atlanta Downtown Ambassador Force, formed during the Olympics to enhance the feeling of safety among tourists. The conservancy trains ambassadors in the history of the park, while the police department trains them in radio usage and polite interactions with the public. Common issues the ambassadors confront are illegal parking, vendors selling without a license, off-leash dogs, and issues such as broken tree limbs. In most cases, the ambassadors can explain to offenders how they are breaking the rules of the park (they also hand out a card listing the park rules) and ask them to comply. The guard is enlisted only if a person refuses to comply, or in cases where professional expertise is advisable. Only in very rare instances would an ambassador contact the police directly—the police have no continuous presence in the park, but send in occasional cycle patrols.

[7] The survey was conducted to determine the views of the public in terms of park strengths, weaknesses, and areas that needed improvement. The 400 user surveys and 400 telephone interviews revealed that many people perceived that there were safety issues connected with the park. A related finding was that most of the park's users were young males and only 11% of users were over age 45.

—— [Chapter 4] ——

Written Agreements

As one might expect, city administrations vary in their approach to sharing responsibility for a piece of the public realm. Some insist on strict guidelines as to the exact roles and responsibilities of the public and private partners. Others allow for a broad, flexible agreement that sketches out general duties. Still other partnerships emerge with no formal agreement at all.

Most nonprofit organizations enter into some form of agreement with their public sector partners to define a mutual working relationship. These agreements go by a number of different names—memoranda of understanding, grant agreements, contracts, and master operating agreements, to name a few. Their main purpose is to recognize the different roles the partners have in the park and the activities they perform, whether they be programming, maintenance, authority over design and capital projects, paying bills, or a combination of all of these. Only in rare cases are these agreements binding contracts that hold the parties responsible to certain standards of upkeep as they would a private contractor. Most often, an MOU or other agreement is a non-binding expression of intent to work together to improve the park. While each agreement is unique to the situation, we can generalize about the basics.

Statement of mission. In the early stages of a partnership, before large-scale capital projects have been identified, and the capacity of the private partner is limited, an agreement might consist only of a joint "statement of mission" for the park acknowledging that the nonprofit has the right to perform certain types of activities in the park like programming, fundraising, or organizing volunteer clean-ups, or granting permits for gatherings and events. At the same time, the agreement will usually establish that the city will be responsible for other activities, such as maintenance or capital funding. Some MOU's in our sample also provide that the parks department will give office space in

a park building to the nonprofit, and allow the group to use the park for appropriate activities.

There is some disagreement in the field about whether or not it is desirable to spell out what specific duties each partner will perform. Many feel that it is better to leave the agreement nonspecific, and therefore flexible and able to accommodate a changing relationship.

Maintenance of Effort. Many MOU's include a "Maintenance of Effort" clause, wherein the parks department agrees to use reasonable effort to maintain the current level of financial commitment to the park during the term of the agreement. Formalizing the public sector's contribution in some way is a significant concern for a nonprofit, because a greater involvement or success in fundraising or caretaking by a private partner may cause the city to feel its commitment can be reduced. In one case in our sample, the nonprofit partner has been so successful at raising funds for the park that it believes the parks department is resentful, and wants to cut the city's annual contribution. We also have encountered many cases where potential funders of nonprofit parks organizations have insisted that the city provide them with an assurance that private support will not replace, but will be supplemental to, sustained public funding.

Operating Subsidies. In certain cases, a city will provide a dedicated annual payment or contribution to a nonprofit for the improvement, maintenance, and/or operation of a park. This payment may be for a limited time, to launch the organization perhaps. It also may take the form of a fee-for-services. For example, as part of their agreement, the city of Richmond, Virginia is obligated to provide at least $125,000 to the Maymont Foundation, and may provide additional funds for improvements, as it chooses (the amount has risen in recent years). The city also provides other services such as tree work. The foundation is authorized to apply for Federal, State or other public funds for the improvement or operation of the park in conjunction with the city. The foundation also receives subsidies from the state of Virginia, and several neighboring counties.

New York City has taken the rare step of formally contracting with the Central Park Conservancy for the management and maintenance of Central Park. The contract provides for the city to pay the conservancy an annual fee-for-services that is determined by a matrix: if the conservancy raises and spends more than $5 million, the city will pay the nonprofit $1 million and match the net increase above $5 million by fifty cents on the dollar. If the conservancy raises over $6 million, the city will also grant the nonprofit 50% of net concession revenues, subject to a cap. Concession monies otherwise go directly into the city's general fund. The arrangement is intended to make it easier for the conservancy to raise money from outside sources, because it can leverage donations off of a city match.

Public review and authority. While the process for determining what is an appropriate activity or alteration to a public park is most often guided by preservation policies, recommendations of an approved master plan, or capital improvements and construction projects that are already planned, the responsibilities of the partners within that process are usually spelled out in an MOU or other agreement. In some cases, a nonprofit organization initiates projects that must be approved by parks departments and other public agencies that have the final authority over capital projects and programs.

Policy and Rules. Concerned with ensuring that parks or greenways remain public places, the public sector commonly retains the power to set and approve policies in the park. Typically these policies are related to operating hours, activities and behavior that is permitted or not permitted, such as the consumption of alcoholic beverages, and the charging of user fees. However, the involvement of the city may also extend to programming and event planning, depending on the situation.

In some cases, the nonprofit organization is given partial or full power to develop and set policies and rules. The Yakima Greenway Foundation, for example, has the power to develop and change policies for the entire greenway. In some cases it follows city and county policies for the land that is within their respective jurisdictions, determining other policies for the greenway as it sees fit. For policies such as the permitting of alcohol and liquor along the greenway, the foundation tends to follow the guidelines set by the city and county. For example, people who wish to rent a covered picnic shelter for a party are required to obtain a state liquor permit. The Maymont Foundation has full rein to set policies for Maymont Estate as long as the park has no admission charge and the majority of the park remains open to the public during normal operating hours.

Transfer of Funds. Sometimes a city and a nonprofit partner will agree that one group or the other will pay for only certain kinds of activities, such as capital projects or a staff member's salary. In these cases, partners may choose to enter into a grant agreement, which allows for one partner to give money, in the form of a grant, to the other for a specific purpose that is its assigned responsibility. The National AIDS Memorial Grove for example, has a grant agreement with the city of San Francisco in which the nonprofit pays for site improvements and construction and, upon their completion, will fund a gardener position in the parks department through an endowment to cover ongoing gardening and maintenance.

No Formal Agreement. Many nonprofits do not have formal written agreements with their partners. Not having a written agreement can be seen to have certain advantages, such as the freedom to operate with considerable flexibility and scope, if one so chooses. Other groups have simply developed working relationships with their public partners that have not necessitated the fashioning of an agreement. Many groups operate for a time without one, but eventually an issue brings the tenuousness of the relationship to bear and an agreement is fashioned. One of our sample organizations that had no agreement with its public sector partner expressed concern that a change in leadership could endanger their partnership, and that a written agreement may be advisable in general.

——— [Chapter 5] ———

The Benefits and Drawbacks of Master Planning

Master plans are tangible and often visible statements of where the park is now, what it should be in the future and what is required to get there. While processes for developing them vary, master plans are most successful when they represent a vision that brings together the concerns of different interest groups, and their recommendations create a ground swell of community and political support. Furthermore, some master plans are less detailed than others, and in some cases, a vision or concept may be adequate, or more desirable.

Good master plans are flexible, and have involved the community and other stakeholders from the outset, giving the plan a legitimate base, and a better chance to come to fruition. While circumstances vary from place to place, the decision to develop a master plan is often determined by the need to understand the current conditions of the park, to generate and build community interest and participation, to create a new and common vision for the park's future, and/or to develop a clear and solid set of recommendations and implementation strategy.

Master plans can build visibility and credibility for a nonprofit group, and can help them target projects and raise money. By the same token, they can call attention to a park's needs and assets and help a parks department or other public agency in their efforts as well. In this way, master plans may be more successful as promotional documents than as blueprints for redesigning a park. Many of our sample organizations worked with, or inherited, master plans from their public sector partners, while several others developed extensive plans of their own.

However, not every group or park needs or would benefit from a master plan. The disadvantages of master plans may include their inflexibility, expense, and the possibility that they may simply sit on a shelf and gather dust. Hiring "experts" such as well-known landscape architects may not guarantee success. In fact, outside experts,

although they can provide an interesting vantage point, can also alienate community members and politicians if they do not include the community's ideas from the beginning.

Master plans commonly include information about the history of the park, the context surrounding its development, and changes that have taken place to the present time. The conditions of existing park facilities, grounds, and landscapes are described and evaluated. People who use the park and live around the park should be interviewed, and should be data gathered to determine who they are, where they go, what they do, what they like and don't like, and what they would like to see changed in the park. Analyses of existing park conditions and the characteristics of park users generally leads to the development of a vision of the park for the future and includes recommendations, plans, designs and strategies for implementation.

While most of the groups we studied have some form of master plan or broad concept plan, the circumstances that brought each one to develop a plan are different. The Friends of Hermann Park, for example, held a national design competition for the northern entrance of the park that revealed larger park-wide issues and problems. Conversely, one of the beginning tasks of the Friends of Buttonwood Park was to help facilitate the creation of the master plan by the city of New Bedford. The Louisville Olmsted Parks Conservancy created its master plan as an early step in its mission to provide a holistic vision for the rehabilitation and management of, and community participation and involvement in, the Olmsted system of parks in Louisville.

Most of the nonprofit organizations in our sample identified the process of developing the master plan as well as the plan itself as being useful for a number of reasons: 1) it challenges the expectations of the general public and public sector about what a park can be and it functions as a vehicle for educating people about park issues; 2)

FRIENDS OF HERMANN PARK

Hermann Park's Grand Basin in the 1990s, and as imagined in a 1995 master plan.

it establishes credibility for the nonprofit; 3) it lays out a work plan for the nonprofit organization; 4) it provides the rationale and framework to raise funds for park needs and specific park projects; and 5) it can be used as a guide for decision-making about park needs and improvements. Another common benefit of the process of master planning is the creation and continuation of a base of active community and political involvement and support for the park and plan.

Building community interest, participation, and consensus as part of the master planning process involves challenging expectations and educating the general public and the public sector about what parks can be. Susan Rademacher, executive director of the Louisville Olmsted Parks Conservancy, had this to say about the process of developing Louisville's master plan:

> . . .When we got started with our master plan, there were a few important things that we focused on. One was that we started with a belief in the native intelligence of this community, from 1888 forward. And we invited the public to really dream about what these parks could be, what they remembered the parks as, and we tried to change expectations in that way. Typically in the past, ...the little changes that come about in parks are politically motivated to get a big bang in the short term for the next election. And ... our parks were suffering from that. So when we invited the community to dream large, we changed the expectations and also changed the expectations of what the public sector was looking to do.

Another outcome of developing a master plan is that it gives organizations credibility. Patricia Winn, formerly the executive director for the Friends of Hermann Park, said; "A vision substantiated by a master plan and backed by funds brought credibility to the group. This made the city take us seriously." The Friends of Hermann Park also hired the landscape architecture firm of Hanna/Olin, which involved park constituencies in the development of a master plan.

For Forest Park Forever, the master plan has not only served as the foundation for building a partnership with the Department of Parks, Recreation, and Forestry, and established a work plan for the partners, but it also provided a basis for fundraising. Jim Mann, executive director of Forest Park Forever, credited the value of a master plan in this way: "By clearly identifying specific capital improvement goals, the master plan has provided a clear agenda for both Forest Park Forever and the parks department. It has also provided tangible goals and capital projects around which we have been able to fundraise and subsequently facilitate implementation." He also stresses the importance of translating future plans for the park into drawings, thereby creating products that people can visualize and grounding ideas and plans in a realistic setting.

Many organizations have found that the creation of a master plan has been useful as a guide for decisions about and/or making changes in, the park. Debbie McCown, executive director of the Piedmont Park Conservancy, noted; "The master plan is our guiding document. City staff and conservancy personnel work closely together to develop working drawings for each project." For the Great Plains Trail Network, the development of a master plan together with the Lincoln/Lancaster Planning Department, city council, and the Recreation Trails Advisory Committee was a critical step, with the result that the city and state now include provisions for trails within their street-improvement and drainage system projects. The plan also "... established a basis for fiscal planning that would support scheduled trail development projects."[8]

However, in other cases, a master plan may be too rigid and "top down" of a strategy to allow for full buy-in from many different organizations, communities or municipalities that may be impacted by a park or open space amenity. In Denver's dense suburbs, the South Suburban Foundation built a greenway through seven towns and several municipalities by keeping its vision simple and flexible, thus allowing for everyone in the county to see connections and other benefits of this "trail," long before it was built. Many towns not even located near the main trail corridor contributed to the effort, convinced of the long-term benefit of the trail, and possible local connector trails to the county and their town. "A detailed master plan would have made our job—to build on the collective imagination of this county— significantly more difficult," said Robert Searns, the greenway consultant for the project.

[8] "American Pathways," National Park Service, 1988, p. 18

How Partnership Organizations are Structured

"The selection of the board is the single most important step in building the long-term health of a nonprofit parks organization," said Tupper Thomas, president of the Prospect Park Alliance. Why? Every nonprofit has a board of directors, and almost every board we studied plays an all-important oversight role that includes setting policies, fundraising and steering the organization to keep it focused on its mission. But this is far from the whole story. Boards take on diverse additional responsibilities according to the needs of each organization, including advocacy, large and small capital projects, publicity, organizing events, design review, planning, development, approving budgets and hiring executive staff members.

The Board

In younger, smaller organizations the board often assumes a hands-on role that is very similar to what staff members do in more established organizations. This is also typical of catalysts and assistance providers, since it is rare that these types of organizations ever develop large staffs. Such boards contribute hands-on management skills and a large amount of time, which is devoted to frequent meetings[9]. Likewise, if an organization is starting up, in a transitional phase, or undertaking a major campaign or project, the board is called on to become more active. This implies that a new organization that has policies to set, money to raise, and little or no staff for day-to-day tasks will put a considerable burden on its board (which may be an argument for evolving an organization and the scope of its responsibilities slowly). The challenge, then, to a new organization, will often be to compose just the right board to ensure its future viability.

Tupper Thomas offers the following advice, "Start out with a powerful board that knows a lot about fundraising. You have to be sure to get some of the more powerful people in the corporate community—some strong donors—and make sure every member of the board is willing to give money at the highest level each is able to give." Indeed, many board members we interviewed told us that they required every member to contribute something to the organization financially, although not everyone could contribute as much as others. Thomas added that, to get a really credible board, it was necessary for her to convince a few key people who move in influential circles to join, and have them recruit the rest of the board members. "Then," adds Thomas, "make time for your board to take some extended time together to make decisions about where you want to go." Board retreats, though resented by some, appear to be a key ingredient in strategic planning for many organizations.

As the organizations we studied aged, their boards tended to withdraw to a more advisory role that focused heavily on fundraising, policy direction, and advising only on the largest capital projects. Says Gregory Platt Jr., president of the Maymont Foundation, "As our organization has grown, the board has moved from organizational and management issues to policy direction and funding." In such more established organizations, the board tended to be bigger, but met less often, probably because they had long since institutionalized the policy and development issues that occupy so much time during an organization's formation.

Not surprisingly, the more the board is relied on for managing and executing day-to-day activities (such as small capital projects, advocacy, publicity) the more frequently it tends to meet. For example, the board of the Louisville Olmsted Parks Conservancy board meets bi-monthly, with some subcommittees meeting every other week to oversee planning and capital improvements. The

---

[9] A unique exception is the South Suburban Park Foundation, which has no staff at all, but subcontracts all project management and construction to consultants, leaving the board free to focus on raising money, identifying partnership opportunities, and reviewing capital projects.

Louisville example illustrates how recruiting professionals to the board, such as architects, lawyers, historic preservationists, and advertising executives, can enhance the organization's staff and almost become an adjunct staff.

Having the support and representation of elected officials as part of a nonprofit's board, plans, and projects was noted as a key factor in enabling many nonprofit organizations to achieve their goals. One nonprofit stated: "By having political representation on the steering committee, the partnership has been able to avoid some bureaucratic difficulties."

Board Composition

Boards usually include those people who have the requisite skills, connections, and financial resources to help the nonprofit achieve its mission. They also usually represent local ethnic groups, community associations, and businesses. Most of the organizations we studied stressed the importance of building a board that represents the full diversity of the area so that all viewpoints are accounted for and to build credibility and contacts among various communities. Ex Officio and/or appointed members often represent the parks department, mayor's office, and city council or affiliate nonprofit groups. These members are important not only because they acknowledge the public sector's role in the park and help legitimize the nonprofit, but they can also provide information otherwise difficult to get and help garner public sector support for projects. If the mission of an organization changes, the board composition may also change with it so that it can address new needs.

The boards we studied varied in size from five to fifty-two, although the size of a board is not necessarily indicative of the size of the organization's staff. Larger boards do seem to be more typical of older organizations. Whatever the board size, its effectiveness ultimately depends on a good understanding of its specific role so that its energies complement the organization's staff and overall needs.

The challenge. . . to a new organization, will often be to compose just the right board to ensure its future viability.

Staffing

The nonprofit organizations we studied varied in staff size from one staff member to 200. In some cases, parks departments provide some administrative help for activities such as routine mailings, preparing minutes, and setting up meetings. Of the organizations we reviewed, just under half employed between two and ten staff persons. About a third of the organizations were volunteer groups or had one staff person, and the remainder had larger staffing levels.

The size of the organization's staff depends upon the type of activities it is engaged in as well as the amount of funding it has. Typically, new organizations begin with volunteers or one or two staff members. In some cases, these groups have one full-time professional staff member who works closely with a board of directors.

Staff levels of organizations that work as catalysts tend to be small as well. While some nonprofits are able to afford from one to four full- or part-time professionals on a staff or consultant basis, others rely solely on volunteers. Regardless of having paid or volunteer staff, these groups regularly make use of volunteers.

Financing A Nonprofit Parks Organization

I n any nonprofit parks enterprise, funding is generally divided into two types: funding for operations and funding for capital projects. Operating funds are those that support the annual budget of the organization that pays for salaries, programs, rent and postage. This budget must somehow be raised every year as long as the organization is in existence. Operating budgets can be as little as a few thousand dollars per year for an assistance provider, or a million or more per year for the largest sole manager and co-manager organizations.

Capital funds, on the other hand, are one-time expenditures used to build (or re-build) a landscape or park facility. Since capital projects are usually bricks and mortar facilities with decades-long lives, the capital budget is generally much larger than a single year's operating budget. On the other hand, a capital fundraising campaign can go on for several years before the funds begin to be spent, without quite the same time pressures to meet payroll and other deadlines that always come with an operating budget. Similarly the spending of a capital budget for the project construction can take several years, depending on the size of the project.

OPERATIONS

Annual operating expenses consist of salaries for employees, office and administrative expenses, publications such as newsletters, expenses associated with fundraising, programs, events, and numerous other recurring costs. If the organization also performs park maintenance or security services through paid employees or contractors, these activities would be major expense items in the operating budget as well.

Size and range of operating budgets. We took a closer look at the operating budgets among our sample of non-profits in order to get a better sense of the relationship between an organization's budget, the types of expenses it has, and the type of role and relationship it has with the public sector. We arranged the organizations into three general budget levels: small ($1,700–$45,000), medium ($100,000–$450,000) and large ($1–$23 million) (See Table 1).

Not surprisingly, those organizations of our nonprofit sample with smaller level operating budgets were those with roles as assistance providers and public advocates, or as catalysts. Smaller level budgets were allocated mainly

TABLE 1.
Grouping of Nonprofits by Operating Budget

Small ($1,700 – $45,000)
Knoxville Greenway Coalition
Friends of Garfield Park
Friends of Buttonwood Park
Great Plains Trail Network
South Suburban Park Foundation

Medium ($100,000 – $450,000)
Louisville Olmsted Parks Conservancy
Piedmont Park Conservancy
Forest Park Forever
National Aids Memorial Grove
Yakima Greenway Foundation

Large ($1 – $23 MILLION)
Central Park Conservancy
Friends of Hermann Park
Maymont Foundation
Partnerships for Parks
Philadelphia Green
Prospect Park Alliance

towards staff salaries and/or administrative costs, fundraising activities, and public programs, events and publications. Three out of four of the organizations within this budget level have volunteer staffs, while only one group, the Friends of Garfield Park, has one regular staff member.

Nonprofits with mid-level operating budgets were mostly those with roles as co-managers, although there were also organizations with roles as catalysts, and as sole managers. Mid-level budgets provide nonprofits with more breathing room, allowing them to allocate more money for administration and professional staff, fundraising, public programs and events, maintenance and operation, public relations, marketing and membership development and services.

Nonprofits with large operating budgets were those with roles as co-managers and sole managers. These larger nonprofits allocate higher levels of funding to the above-mentioned areas and branch out further into visitor services and facilities rental. The Maymont Foundation, the primary caretaker for Maymont, a public park that was a private estate, allocates money to the maintenance and operation of facilities within the park, including a museum, carriage collection, nature center, and a farm with animals.

Revenues. Finding funds to cover the annual operating budget is one of the biggest challenges facing parks nonprofit organizations, all of whom derive their funding from six different sources: 1) government subsidies; 2) private donations and contributions (individual and corporate); 3) foundation grants; 4) concessions or other earned income sources; 5) in-kind contributions; and 6) earned interest from investments and/or an endowment.

Often the first source is in-kind contributions — ranging from volunteer time to donated office space to public service announcements in the media. For the purposes of this chapter, however, we will be discussing sources of cold, hard cash to pay the bills — cash that has to be raised every year to keep the organization going.

Occasionally there is endowment income as well — the product of funds invested for the income they can produce every year (interest, dividends and capital gains) to replace annual

fundraising. However, an endowment to support operations (as opposed to a facility) is produced only through an enormous fund raising campaign that is unlikely to be undertaken, let alone successful, until an organization is large, well-established, and seen by funders as a credible long-term steward of capital.

In our research we found that local foundations were likely to be among the first funding sources for a new organization. National foundations eventually might be attracted to an effective organization, especially if its activities fall within one of the foundation's program categories. Local foundations are often approached for seed money and start up grants, as well as capital campaigns, although they may ask to have their funds "matched" by other monies from other sources. This may be when the organization turns to individuals, as well as corporations.

Individuals are another common source of cash for a new organization, often through the vehicle of membership dues, but also through larger contributions from those who care passionately about the park and also have the ability contribute at a higher level. Individuals are often the source of funds secured through fundraising events. Sales of t-shirts, hats, and other items also can generate funds from individuals. Some groups have extensive catalogs of ways for individuals to invest in parks, and will let people sponsor everything from a waste receptacle to a child's term in a summer camp program.

Private corporations, especially those with developed corporate giving programs and/or an office near the park, are another likely source of funds, especially if some of their employees become part of the parks organization. Initially these businesses may give small contributions, but their donations can be potentially very large, especially when the park is seen as having a major effect on the corporation's image.

The three sources discussed above are all private-sector sources. To access them, the parks organization almost surely will need to have a tax-exempt designation (under Section 501(c)(3) of the U.S. Internal Revenue Code). This designation, which can be obtained by application to the U.S. Internal Revenue Service demonstrating that the organization's purposes are charitable, religious or educational, will qualify funds as a tax deduction for the donor (a significant incentive in the case of individuals and corporations), or—in the case of a foundation—as an eligible candidate for its charitable funds. It is this ability to access private funding that makes a nonprofit partner attractive to a municipal parks department, and gives it an incentive to match the private funds the nonprofit raises. Some groups use the tax-exempt designation of a third party, although as they mature, they usually achieve their own designation.

Government sources are most likely to come in the form of a contract for services with the municipal government, usually specifying what services the nonprofit will perform in support of the park, and often with a budget specified. A government, usually city or county, also might make an outright grant to support the organization.

Earned income can include rentals paid by outside vendors of park facilities that the organization controls, such as food facilities, skating rinks, docks, or just space for a business to operate. Needless to say, such businesses should all complement and enhance the park; in fact this might be the first objective of such concessions, with the income used just to cover their costs.

Earned income also can come from recreational program fees, event admissions and gift or souvenir sales, among others. One group among many in our sample highlighted opportunities to earn rental income from the buildings that they have renovated and continue to manage. Depending on the location of the park, and especially the amount of pedestrian traffic near it, earned income can be considerable.

An entrepreneurial organization with a well thought out leasing plan that programs and animates park spaces into a synergistic whole can go far towards changing the park's image and revitalizing it. Since nonprofits can generally be more entrepreneurial and flexible than government agencies, possibly earning a surplus where a city

If the nonprofit is able to get control of the concessions and recycle the income into its own budget, this can be a substantial, stable, and long-term source of operating income.

could not, the parks department may be willing to cede some control through a contractual arrangement if it is seen to be in the best interest of the park. If the nonprofit is able to get control of the concessions and recycle the income into its own budget, this can be a substantial, stable, and long-term source of operating income. Concession services might also be run directly by the organization, but then it must provide the expertise and absorb the expenses as well; generally leasing out to experts is preferable.

In summary, it is worth noting that an important goal for any nonprofit organization, especially if it aspires to a long life as a park steward, is to maintain diverse and balanced funding using all these sources for its operating budget. Then, the shrinkage or disappearance of any one source will not spell the end of the organization's existence or effectiveness.

CAPITAL PROJECTS

Capital expenses refer to the one-time cost of creating an asset—usually a park or park facility (although the term can also refer to the building of an endowment). These costs generally include not only the "hard costs" of construction materials and labor, but also the "soft costs" of design, insurance, legal services, project management, and any other needs necessary to see the project through implementation. The initial conception and planning of a new capital project, however, might need to be carried in the operating budget: the staffing of a planning committee, the hiring of a planner or designer to do the first concept drawings, the development of renderings to communicate a vision of the project, and cost estimates to put a price tag on it. This work provides a basis for raising capital funds. Once some or all the funds are raised, however, the subsequent management of the project can be justified and should be provided for in the capital budget itself.

As the planning for a capital project progresses, the skills required become increasingly specialized and technical, and the liability issues much greater. Unless the nonprofit organization is very sophisticated or has its own knowledgeable client representative, the legal responsibility for implementation of a capital project may well pass to the parks department or to another government agency, with the nonprofit serving as a junior partner and fundraiser.

Revenues. Because capital projects almost always result in the construction of a public space or public facility, and because they generally constitute very large expenditures-often dwarfing the yearly operating budget of a nonprofit-a large percentage of the funds to pay for them usually come from public sources. City, county, state, or federal funds—or some mix of these—will probably account for the bulk of the capital funding for park projects. However, a nonprofit's ability to raise private funds is one of the biggest points of leverage in its partnership with the city. Capital funds, whether public or private, almost always are designated for a specific project, or group of projects.

In-kind contributions also can play a significant role in a capital project, whether they are donated architectural services, contributed construction materials, or pro bono legal or construction management services. Adopt-a-tree and adopt-a-bench programs are also popular ways of generating individual support, as are "brick" campaigns, where donors are asked to buy a brick or other paving block.

In addition, an endowment can be raised to ensure the long-term maintenance and care of a capital facility. Sometimes an endowment is raised as part of the initial capital campaign that pays for building the facility; more often it is raised as part of a campaign to fund the rehabilitation of a deteriorated and beloved landmark. Endowments typically will be raised from private sources. The yearly income from the endowment is earmarked for regular maintenance and repair, or for capital replacement of the designated asset(s).

Building a Nonprofit Parks Organization

The people who run nonprofit parks organizations today have been an invaluable source of information for this book. We have taken some of their ideas and wisdom and have developed the following composite of the keys to success in building an effective nonprofit parks organization. These keys range from information on starting up and hands-on advice to insights from work in different parts of the country.

Understand the playing field before you begin.
Developing and shaping the role of a nonprofit organization usually starts with defining what is currently lacking in the park or greenway or municipality (probably the issues that brought a group together in the first place) within the context of other organizations involved in the area or park, the roles that these other groups play, and how well they perform them. Identifying who and what responsibilities the involved public agencies, community groups, and other nonprofits assume in the park or greenway helps pinpoint where, in these relationships, a particular organization might be most needed. This kind of analysis of other efforts should include an assessment of whether they are being done effectively or not.

Develop an effective, focused community process.
Agreeing on a participatory and formal process to involve neighborhood groups and key elected officials at the outset of a working relationship builds community involvement, stewardship, more responsive design or programming, and political support. One organization noted: "...outreach and inclusiveness in the plan development process.... increases trust and legitimacy in the surrounding communities." Another group said: "Good communication and the involvement and 'buy in' of key players (the movers and shakers) to the importance of the project has enabled the partnership to achieve its goals."

Identify the assets of the community. Well beyond the "stakeholders" described above—the parks, planning and public works departments, for example—there are hundreds of groups and people in every city who could be associated with the park in some way, but aren't. Many of these are organizations that currently use the park, including sports leagues, exercise groups, dog walkers, bird watchers, chess clubs, and countless others. In addition there are probably many individual park users who know a great deal about what happens in the park because they use it every morning, when they walk their dog, or every evening, when they meet friends. These users exist in every park and are invaluable as a resource.

There are also many groups that would like to be able to use the park, but don't for any number of reasons, including complex city permitting, concern for safety, or simple lack of knowledge about the park and what it could offer them. All of these types of users, current and potential, need to become a part of the "assets inventory" so that they can be given an opportunity to become future users and supporters. "Involving the community in the planning and implementation effort is not only wise, it is necessary for success," said Tupper Thomas, administrator of Prospect Park in Brooklyn.

Develop a vision. A vision for the park or greenway that is flexible enough to change and realistic to the extent that it is feasible will, in the long run, facilitate a coordinated park strategy and build in support for park plans, programs, and projects. Many nonprofits noted that the development of a "master plan" was an important factor that enabled programs and projects to get underway. Whether or not a master plan exists, a vision that evolves from a community process is essential. The benefits and liabilities associated with master planning are discussed in Chapter 5.

Gauge the Capacity of the Nonprofit Organization.
The role of the organization should reflect the
group's capability. Many of the groups presented
here began with small, defined roles, but had big
visions and dreams. The roles grew along with
the capacity of their organizations as they proved
themselves and gathered momentum. Once the
"missing link" in the playing field was determined,
the ability of the organization to fill the gaps can
be evaluated.

While every situation is different, the general steps
in assessing an organization's capacity are:

1. Begin by determining the tasks and activities
   that may be required for the organization in
   order to carry out its role.
2. Consider the staff and or people that will be
   needed in the day-to-day operation of the
   organization and whether the organization
   can be adequately staffed for the work
   required.
3. Think about whether the leadership, staff,
   board, and/or volunteers have the skills or
   knowledge required.
4. Determine whether the budget and funding
   of the organization will allow it to carry out
   these activities.

Maintain a clear focus. Some of our interviews suggested that one of the key mistakes of nonprofits
involved in parks is to take on too many activities,
rather than focusing only on those that achieve
the mission. In some cases, involvement in these
activities has overextended the capacity and ability
of the organization to staff and perform them well.

Limiting the roles of the organization at first
can work to a nonprofit's advantage, as working
relationships and partnerships only develop once
a group has demonstrated its capabilities and built
trust over time. For new groups, this may mean
taking on small projects like clean-ups to begin
with and formalizing a relationship with the parks
department much later. The exception to this rule
is when the public sector takes the lead in establishing a nonprofit and contributes start-up money
and expertise to do so.

A more informal and flexible working relationship is often particularly important for both non-

profits and the public sector to achieve their goals
while they are in the process of developing a new
working partnership. One nonprofit recommended: "Start slowly, maintain flexibility, and don't be
too structured until you know exactly what needs
to be achieved for success." However, some feel
that being involved in a broad range of activities
has been important in putting forth an inclusive,
more responsible management mission.

Define a realistic mission statement. The mission
of the organization should largely reflect or define
the activities it gets involved in. The mission statements of all 15 organizations in our sample can
be found in the case studies that follow in the next
section.

Cultivate the public/private relationship. Although
the relationship between the public and private
sector is different in every city, all groups must regularly work with, or in support of, their partners.
Some have fostered this relationship by locating
in the same building or office, believing that a
close working environment allows for ongoing
mutual support and an open attitude toward solv-
ing problems as they arise. When the nonprofit
has a good relationship and rapport with the park
staff, especially park gardeners and maintenance
workers, the result, more often that not, is trust
and respect, a mutual understanding of park
issues, and better park care. Some groups take it
upon themselves to recognize park workers regularly, holding barbecues, awards ceremonies, training seminars, or other events just for maintenance
or recreation staff.

Some organizations build a relationship with
the parks department into their organizational
structure through the joint appointment of a staff
member, typically their president, as a staff member of the parks department or other city agency,
as well. This practice has the added effect of rein-
forcing the "public" aspect of the park, because
it allows the director to balance competing issues.
In contrast, without this perception, a strong nonprofit may be seen as overly responsive to its
donors, and less so to the public in general.

On the other hand, nonprofits also feel that
an important aspect of the working relationship is
the freedom, independence, and lack of interfer-

ence from city agencies to operate and manage the park. These organizations tend to be nonprofit organizations that are primary care givers for the park who prefer to have the independence to manage and maintain the park facilities as they see fit. One nonprofit commented: "Our experience is that the total independence we have in operations is the cleanest way to work. The onus is on us to raise the money, but we know if we do there is no bureaucratic interference in how it is spent." Another way of getting more autonomy is through additional activities, like maintenance, because the more these groups are doing, the less they have to ask for from the parks department. However, eventually this dynamic will reach a point where the public vs. private question will come up.

Select the right projects. Many groups we spoke to told us that the best way they found to develop credibility was to start with short-term, yet inspiring projects that could be completed within a few years or less. Completing projects on time, within a budget and honoring commitments made to public and private sector donors help to enhance credibility, especially for longer-term capital projects.

Tupper Thomas, of the Prospect Park Alliance, described this issue perfectly. "For a first project, you have to pick something that can be done pretty quickly and that can be very well received. Pick a good sexy project. We selected to renovate our carousel for about $700,000. The carousel was a good selection because it was visible and it didn't cost so much that it was impossible to raise the money, but it was nonetheless impressive and very challenging, it had naming opportunities (each horse could be bought), it had a great history, there was nothing controversial about it, it was a popular amenity, and it created a new destination in the park. We also discovered that foundations liked it for the same reasons."

Make a long-term commitment. Many groups expressed the importance of having a long-term view and emphasized that the public sector and

A strong board provides critical expertise, leadership, and fundraising for nonprofit organizations.

the nonprofit should both commit themselves to long-term involvement. The financial commitment ensures that both partners have a stake in the project and provides a real incentive to achieve a successful outcome. Having its own money invested enables the nonprofit to move ahead with plans and projects and not just talk about it. The necessity of both partners to commit to a long-term relationship also was seen as important. The director of one nonprofit said: "Partnerships need to realize and expect the long term commitment that is necessary to accomplish the tasks at hand. It is this long term commitment that is often lacking in grassroots organizations."

Recruit a strong board. A strong board provides critical expertise, leadership, and fundraising for nonprofit organizations. A diversity of talent in the areas in which the nonprofit expects to be most active—such as fundraising and capital projects-and ex-officio representation from the public sector partners, are all key aspects of board selection. Many of the organizations we interviewed described their boards in different ways; in some cases the board actually functioned as the staff of the organization. Many groups noted that the selection of their board was the most important step in determining the health and long-term effectiveness of their organization.

—[**Part II**]—

The Partnership Organizations

The practice of augmenting, or even replacing, public commitments to parks and open space with private funds is not without controversy. Many citizens feel that they have a right to expect clean, safe parks and downtowns as "basic public services." This expectation stems naturally from the previous commitments our city governments made to parks in the last century. However, at some point every city asks itself what the acceptable levels of cleanliness and safety should be and how relevant they are as measurements of a park's success if the park is not also well used and loved by its citizenry. They must ask this question, in part because many parks and other public spaces are indeed clean and safe, but are also empty and devoid of life.

To address this issue, different cities have accepted different combinations of public and private funds and efforts in managing, maintaining, programming, and fundraising for their public parks. These unique mixtures reflect a metropolitan area's individuality, and its social and political mores. There is no perfectly replicable approach to public private partnerships in this area, or perhaps any area. Each city must chart its own course.

Public private partnerships can take many forms. There are cities and municipalities that allow their citizens the opportunity to invest in their public spaces in any way they can, maintaining nearly complete public support in the process. However, while every city government may feel obligated to manage its public spaces, it is sometimes both more efficient and more rational to offer the programming and management of that space, be it a park or a main street or a public market, to a different organization, perhaps a group of interested volunteers, or even a private management company that must answer to the city.

Some of these partner organizations are small nonprofit volunteer groups with an ability to funnel tax-deductible donations into a city park. However many groups go far beyond that function, organizing volunteers, advocating for open space,

The key element in the establishment of these partnerships, and the key variable for their success, is leadership.

running educational and other programs, and providing security. Other groups, in advocating for new spaces, take the lead in building coalitions and creating designs for new parks. Still other groups are huge management and maintenance organizations with professional gardeners and landscapers, architects and planners, who are contracted with to oversee nearly every aspect of a park's management and growth.

For all these reasons—additional funds, stewardship, efficiency of operation, increased access to volunteers, increased pressure to create and properly manage open spaces—nearly every city in the country has attempted some kind of public/private partnership. But the truly successful partnership models are the ones where the city has sought a solution for its parks and its neighborhoods with this single community partnership mechanism.

For what many people involved in managing parks come to realize is that involving people in the creation of a true "place" can—if it is done with full participation and a genuine interest and willingness to incorporate people's desires and ideas into a design scheme—result in precisely the stewardship over the space that is the ultimate goal of any management organization. This is because these are the only real factors that will decrease crime and increase cleanliness in a sustainable way.

These new roles for the nonprofit sector have evolved over the last 30 years as the concept of parks has changed along with the willingness of city governments and policymakers to see parks and open spaces as having the potential to renew neighborhoods and downtowns. Often it has taken the influence of visionary private citizens to make this leap. Sometimes it is the city government that takes the lead in organizing a study to determine the viability of a nonprofit role in parks management and assistance. Either way, the key element in the establishment of these partnerships, and the key variable for their success, as the following case studies will show, is leadership.

Friends of Buttonwood Park

New Bedford, MA

The origins of the Friends of Buttonwood Park are in statewide rather than local activism. In 1983 the Massachusetts Association for Olmsted Parks conducted a pilot study of public parks in the state that had been designed by Frederick Law Olmsted and his firm, including Buttonwood Park. The organization hoped to create a model Olmsted park inventory that could be useful nationwide.

Of the more than 280 public parks designed by the Olmsted firm in Massachusetts, the study highlighted ten parks it felt demonstrated a representative sample of both the range and condition of the Olmsted parks in Massachusetts. New Bedford's Buttonwood Park was on the list. According to the inventory, Buttonwood Park's trees "suffered from vandalism and neglect," its buildings were "poorly maintained," and the sporadic additions of recreation facilities and parking have caused the park to lose definition and character.[11]

In producing the report, the association's members hoped that they would bring attention to these valuable landscapes, and also help locate the money needed to rehabilitate them. The report had the desired effect. Influenced by the study, the Massachusetts Department of Environmental Management created a program called the Olmsted Historic Landscape Preservation Program, and in 1987 the department funded studies and rehabilitation projects for 15 parks in Massachusetts, including Buttonwood Park, which was awarded $1.2 million.

The mayor of New Bedford appointed 32 residents, including members of the parks department, to form a citizens advisory committee that would guide the development of a master plan, funded by a grant from the Massachusetts Department of Environmental Management. The committee hired a consultant to prepare the plan, which covered the concerns outlined by the inventory report and also raised other important issues such as flooding, vehicle congestion, safety, and

the need for ongoing management and maintenance. It also recommended that a friends group be formed to "provide overview of and support for the park."[12]

Later that year, the citizen's advisory committee formed the Friends of Buttonwood Park to oversee the master plan's implementation. The new group entered into a cooperative agreement with the Department of Environmental Management and the city of New Bedford, the two key partners in this project to date. The New Bedford Zoological Society, which managed the Buttonwood Zoo, offered to serve as an umbrella organization for the friends; the president of the society helped the friends to develop a set of by-laws, obtain 501(c)3 status, and form an organization in nine months. The initial members set about developing a wider membership for the friends by holding public meetings and inviting speakers, including Tupper Thomas of the Prospect Park Alliance, and Betsy Shure-Gross, co-chair of the National Association of Olmsted Parks.

Formed to assume a watchful eye over the master plan and the park, the friends oversaw the first round of capital improvements in the park based on the plan. One million dollars from the Department of Environmental Management grant was spent on building a great lawn (part of the original Olmsted, Olmsted and Eliot plan that was never implemented), a pedestrian walkway through the park with benches and lights, and on recon-

---

[10] McPeck, Eleanor M.; Morgan, Keith; and Zaitzevsky, Cynthia, editors; Brookline, Mass. 1983, "Olmsted in Massachusetts: the Public Legacy: A Report of the Inventory Committee of the Massachusetts Association for Olmsted Parks," p 37.

[11] Walker-Kluesing Design Group. (1987). Reclaiming the Useable Past: A Master Plan for Veteran's Memorial Park and Zoo at Buttonwood Park, New Bedford, Massachusetts. Prepared under the Olmsted Historic Landscape Preservation Program, Massachusetts Department of Environmental Management, Contract No. 251-85, Executive Summary Section, page 1.

Buttonwood Park | New Bedford, MA

AT APPROXIMATELY 98 acres, Buttonwood Park is one of New Bedford's largest and most heavily used parks. The famous landscape architecture firm of Olmsted, Olmsted and Eliot designed the park in 1895 in their characteristic naturalistic landscape style, with a large pond, stream, groves, lawns, and a forest. However, the original plan was never fully implemented. A 1987 master plan noted that "Buttonwood Park's 90-year evolution has been piecemeal and sporadic, providing services and facilities as needs have arisen ."[12] At that time, there were several park facilities, including 10 tennis courts, three ballfields, three basketball courts, an exercise room, a zoo, a library, a greenhouse, a nursery, a bandshell, a Veterans Memorial Building, a warming house, 12 monuments, and five parking areas. A decade ago, the city initiated renovations on the park. A great lawn and a pedestrian promenade, based on the Olmsted firm's original design, were added. More recently, several maintenance buildings have been demolished. Buttonwood Park is listed on the National Register of Historic Places.

Located in a residential area of the city of New Bedford, Massachusetts, the park is bordered by city streets and surrounded by houses built between 1910 and 1930. Residents are predominantly middle class and are culturally diverse. In addition to the wide range of facilities that the park has to offer, the Buttonwood Park Zoo attracts both residents and visitors to New Bedford. The park is host to the city's annual Whaling Festival, a three-day event that attracts over 300,000 people.

structing tennis courts that had been eliminated to allow for the great lawn. A new playground, another improvement recommended in the master plan, was added with money raised by an independent group that later joined the friends.

Though their influence is strongly felt in the city, the friends are a small organization. In conjunction with their role as the stewards of the master plan, the friends focus on park programming, organizing volunteers, and advocacy. Programming activities include concerts, and providing and maintaining an outdoor reading space in conjunction with the public library. Volunteers serve as the staff of the friends organization and are also involved in park clean-ups, tree maintenance, and staffing activities and programs. The volunteer board runs the group on a tiny $3,500 annual operating budget. The New Bedford Department of Parks and Recreation maintains and manages the park.

However, defining the friends' role, as well as

their working relationship with the parks department has not been all smooth sailing. In 1994, several years after the great lawn and promenade had been built, the U.S. Department of Agriculture issued a formal complaint about the severe deficiencies at the New Bedford Zoo. The city took an aggressive approach to revitalization that included plans for a significant expansion into the park, and the addition of 250 parking spaces. The friends became concerned—the expansion would clearly impinge heavily upon the master plan for the park and would require significant alterations to improvements that were already in place.

Committed to a public process, the board of the Friends of Buttonwood Park brought their concerns to the parks department and told them that they wanted to hold public meetings about the zoo expansion and its impact on the park. The parks department, the zoological society, and the friends

[12] Walker-Kluesing Design Group, 1987, ibid.

hosted the workshops and public meetings collectively, with the understanding that it was important for the groups to get along. Compromise did not come easily, but eventually limitations were placed on the zoo expansion, although parts of the new pedestrian concourse would have to be replaced, and 135 parking spaces, rather than 250, are now in the main parking lot. As a result of this process, according to Jean Bennett, president of the Friends of Buttonwood Park, "the friends emerged stronger and more respected by the parks department."

The friends have been involved in other advocacy issues as well, including a campaign to create and implement a pooper-scooper law, and an effort to limit the number of additional memorial statues in the park by encouraging people to plant trees instead. The friends also have been very involved in advocating for the city's annual Whaling Festival to be relocated from the park to an alternate location, and promoting increased and safe use of the park. The friends also raise funds for park events and capital improvements. In 1998, the friends raised approximately $10,000 in revenue from contributions, including those to their tree fund.

In addition to increasing their current activities in the next few years, the friends plan to expand their park involvement to include security, design and planning for capital improvements, marketing and outreach, and remedial maintenance. While the parks department and the New Bedford Zoological Society are the sole managers for the park and the zoo, the friends have hopes of expanding their working partnership with the city to become more actively involved in managing and maintaining the park in the future.

Mobilizing the community is a key activity for the Friends of Buttonwood Park.

Name of Park: Buttonwood Park

Location: New Bedford, Massachusetts

Size: 98 acres

Primary Caretaker: New Bedford Department of Parks and Recreation

Name of Organization: Friends of Buttonwood Park

Type: Assistance Provider and Public Advocate

Mission: The Friend's mission is to work with the community in support of all efforts to preserve and promote Buttonwood Park as a premier horticultural and zoological landscape. The Friends work to provide the public with information, rest, relaxation, and recreation in Buttonwood Park and assist governmental agencies to enable people to enjoy the park in peace and safety.

Staff: None

Board: 18 members (maximum is not to exceed 30); Ex Officio: New Bedford Zoological Society, the Park Board /Department and one city representative as appointed by the Mayor.

Master Plan: 1987

Written Agreements: MOU

Contact
Jean Bennett, President
Friends of Buttonwood Park
P.O. Box 2011
New Bedford, MA 02741
(508) 996-9130

www.newbedford.com/buttonwood

Friends of Garfield Park, Inc.

Indianapolis, Indiana
Garfield Park has a long history of volunteerism. From its earliest days in 1873, immigrant volunteers flocked to the new park's greenhouses to plant and care for species native to their homelands. However, for most of its existence Garfield Park did not have its own nonprofit or community group to organize and represent park users.

In the 1980s, Garfield Park suffered a fate similar to many urban parks in the United States—severe budget cuts forced maintenance cutbacks in the Indianapolis Parks Department, and Garfield Park was neglected. Eventually, it's pool leaked, its playgrounds were unsafe, and the park had developed a well-deserved reputation as a center of illicit activity-in 1990, more vice arrests occurred in Garfield than in any other park in the system, according to Mark Bowell, the former director of the Indianapolis Parks Foundation. Several years later, Mayor Stephen Goldsmith hired Leon

Younger, formerly the director of parks and recreation in Jackson County/Kansas City, Missouri to oversee a long-term plan to revitalize the Indianapolis Parks System. The focus was on establishing a plan to increase community outreach and earned income, large citywide meetings were held and the mayor promised that $10 million from a bond campaign would go toward park improvements. The park eventually received $5 million of that money, and in 1996 was able to restore its conservatory, swimming pool, playground, and pagoda. However, when the mayor ran for governor and lost, the program lost momentum.

Soon thereafter, the state of Indiana pledged $500,000 for the park, and the Lilly Endowment stepped forward with $4 million towards restoration of the park's historic Sunken Garden, and for construction of a new recreation facility. But Lilly was skeptical that the community was fully behind the changes in the park, and wanted a reassurance

DAN FRANCIS, MARDAN PHOTOGRAPHY

Garfield Park's Sunken Garden, designed by George Kessler, was renovated in the late 1990s.

Garfield Park | Indianapolis, Indiana

IT SEEMS APPROPRIATE that first park in Indianapolis, the home of the country's most famous motor speedway, began as a racetrack. Indeed, the area known as Garfield Park today was originally a horseracing facility built by the Indianapolis Fair Association in the 1850's. Ironically, the track was a failure, and the association sold the land to the city in 1873. The 128-acre site was the first piece of property the city bought specifically to develop as a public park.

The park's roots are in its greenhouses. Twenty years after the site was acquired by the city, the park had 40,000 square feet of greenhouse space. The park supplied plantings for most of the major civic institutions in town, but, more significantly, it provided a community gardening program of some magnitude - all the plantings in and maintenance of the facility was done by volunteers. By the turn of the 20th century, greenhouse space had expanded to nearly 200,000 square feet.

In 1908, George Kessler, a landscape architect and onetime Olmsted protégé, who was developing a scheme for parks and boulevards throughout Indianapolis, designed Garfield Park. Kessler had a prolific career, eventually planning the park systems of Kansas City, Denver and nearly a dozen other Midwestern cities, as well as parkways and individual parks in dozens of cities and states across the country. He designed Garfield Park in a more formal style, emphasizing the greenhouse's function by building a large glass conservatory, now the central feature of the park, and a classical sunken garden, though he also left large wooded areas and open meadows in the park.

In addition to the 7,500 square foot conservatory and the four-acre Sunken Garden, Garfield Park now also includes several monuments and memorials, a performing arts center, a family and aquatic center, a pagoda, a trail and bike system, numerous playgrounds, ballfields, and several tennis courts.

both that capital improvements were being prioritized correctly and that the park's maintenance would be adequately funded into the future. Therefore, the foundation placed a condition on the grant-it mandated that an organization be formed that could both provide a forum for the residents to express their priorities for the park, and endow its maintenance into the future. With help from the Indianapolis Parks Foundation, the Friends of Garfield Park was initiated in 1998 by members of the foundation and local residents who had been active in the planning of the park from the outset. The friends convened the communities surrounding the park through their neighborhood associations, churches, schools, politicians, businesses, and merchants. They came up with a list of priorities for Garfield Park and began to raise the necessary money to endow maintenance.

According to Mark Bowell, who is now the friends' development consultant, the organization's primary role is to raise a $3 million endowment for the continued maintenance of the park's conservatory, which was rebuilt in the 1950's, and the sunken garden, which was completely restored in 1998 with the funds from the Lilly Endowment.

Bowell notes that the endowment is not about alleviating the commitment of the public sector. The friends have a specific maintenance of effort clause in their memorandum of understanding with the parks department (see Chapter 4, Written Agreements) that holds the city commitment to

Garfield Park to at least the 1997 budgetary level. "The endowment is a safety net," says Bowell, "it allows us to provide the value added funds the department needs to keep the park to the highest standards."

The friends organize two main fundraising campaigns, one for their operating costs, and one for the endowment. Last year's effort raised approximately $150,000 for the organization, and they have established a goal of $365,000. In the endowment campaign, their goal over four years is to raise $3 million. The friends have been given the right to use naming opportunities as fundraising tools only for the Sunken Garden, and offer bricks, fountains and other amenities for people to adopt. They would like to expand that right to include the entire park in the future, however the naming opportunities are still restricted to amenities - donors cannot adopt an entire area of the park.

The friends also have a goal of increasing community input into park planning. To that end, they have established a twice-yearly event, known as the "Friends Forum" to elicit suggestions and get feedback from local park users and organizations. The first event, held in May, 2000, attracted over 200 people, and the friends needed to rent a tent to accommodate them. The friends also provided food and entertainment. "It's a check and balance thing," says Bowell. "We find out from the neighbors and stakeholders whether we're doing our job."

The friends' offices are located at the Garfield Park Conservatory, and they share space with the Friends of Garfield Park Conservatory, an all-volunteer group that runs a plant shop on site.

Although it is a major piece of the Indianapolis parks system, Garfield Park does not have a master plan. However, the board of the friends is working on a strategic plan for the group, and the parks department is currently developing a comprehensive five-year plan.

Name of Park: Garfield Park

Location: Indianapolis, Indiana

Park Size: 128 acres

Primary Caretaker: Indianapolis Department of Parks and Recreation

---

Name of Organization: Friends of Garfield Park, Inc.

Type of Organization: Assistance Provider

Year Formed: 1998

Staff: 2

Board: 12 members

Mission: "The mission of the Friends of Garfield Park, Inc is to ensure the preservation and continuation of public benefits of Garfield Park through enhanced funding, the application of effective advocacy, and expanded stewardship."

Master Plan: None

Written Agreements: MOU, 1999

Contact
Mark Bowell
The Friends of Garfield Park
2345 Pagoda Drive
Indianapolis, IN
317.327.7336
mbowell@imcpl.lib.in.us

——————[**Assistance Provider**]——————

Great Plains Trail Network

Lincoln, Nebraska

One would suspect that people in Nebraska would intuitively understand that trails can help build cities. As thousands of settlers streamed from East to West in the 1840's along the Oregon Trail, and 1850's, forts and towns in Nebraska were established to serve them. Thus, trails made Nebraska grow. In time, these well-worn trails were replaced by railroads, and later, by the interstate. Although Route 80 cuts a wide gash through the southern portion of the state, railroad lines, many long abandoned, still connect the towns to one another, and provide a perfect network of linkages and trails to help build Nebraska's settled areas, instead of simply helping people pass through the state on their way someplace else.

There was little recognition of the potential for a trail network in the Lincoln area until 1987. It was then, at the behest of the city planning department, that the city engaged in a strategic planning effort to discover what people wanted Lincoln to look like in the future. Called "Star Venture," the meetings convened over 100 citizens to discuss Lincoln and its future growth. One participant was Elaine Hammer, a long-time member of the city planning commission, fresh off a formative experience—riding over Vail Pass in Colorado with her sister and son. "From that experience, I saw what a tremendous asset trails could be to a community," said Hammer. She co-chaired a committee on the strategic planning team and, as a result, a trail network was adopted as a key goal of the Star Venture effort.

The city planning director liked the idea, and later that year approached Hammer to help bring it about. There was a bond measure brewing to raise money to restore a children's zoo, and it made sense to try to raise some funds for trail development along with it. Hammer quickly realized that she would have to mobilize people to get the measure passed, so in May, 1988 she formed the Great Plains Trail Network, and began to search for a trail constituency.

Hammer approached leaders from fitness groups such as bicyclists and runners, neighborhood groups, planners, and health industry specialists such as physical therapists and physicians.

Lincoln Mayor Mike Johanns rides across the new Highway 2 bridge.

Lincoln Area Trail System | Lincoln, Nebraska

THE LINCOLN AREA Network consists of 78 miles of trails in and around the city of Lincoln, Nebraska. The trails run primarily along abandoned railways, bridges, and drainage channels; others are located within residential neighborhoods, near business areas, parks, country woodlands, and farmlands. Trails are typically 8-10 feet wide and have hard surfaces of concrete, asphalt, or crushed limestone. The trail surfaces support a range of activities: most prominently walking, hiking, jogging, biking, and in-line skating.

With an economy based primarily on white-collar jobs in light industries such as insurance, a state university, several small colleges, and county and state government, Lincoln has an ethnically and economically diverse population of approximately 200,000.

Rather than asking for money, she asked them to be on the board of her new organization. The city demonstrated it's support for a trail network by developing a master plan, and acquiring an abandoned railroad corridor from the former Rock Island Line. In November 1989, the bond measure passed resoundingly. "In the end," says Hammer proudly, "the trail carried the zoo."

The group was tested quickly when 25 miles of abandoned railroad easements became available shortly after the bond measure passed. Hammer approached the Natural Resource District, a regional governmental administration with a recreation portfolio, to help obtain the corridor for use as a trail. The District told Hammer they would manage the trail once it acquired, but that she would have to find a way to purchase the land.

At first, Hammer approached a friend at a large local bank for funds. In a rare show of audacity, eight couples, including Hammer, borrowed the $375,000 from the bank against their own property and bought the land for the trail. "That strongly motivated us to find donors," Hammer half-joked. When a corporate contact told her that corporations wouldn't give to her organization until it had proved itself by raising money on its own, Hammer and her board went out to the doctors and bicyclists and runners to raise the first $100,000. "Doctors are a beautiful source of funds for a trail," she notes.

Once the first $100,000 was raised, the group returned to the corporations, who came up with

the rest of the $375,000. Since that first success, GPTN has focused hard on continued acquisition and development of new trails in the Lincoln area. There are now 78 miles of trails in the area. Hammer estimates that there were ten when the group began.

With a current membership of 800, the Network is heavily involved in organizing volunteers and assisting other trail organizations across the state. GPTN and local agencies often sponsor events such as walks, runs and in-line skating on the trails and help with the publicity, registration and monitoring of these events. Money raised from event entrance fees, t-shirts, raffles, and other such sales go toward trail enhancements. GPTN board members also provide on-going direction for the organization, produce a newsletter, and conduct direct mailings. The GPTN is less involved in the designing and planning of trail capital improvements.

Occasionally, the goals of the group and that of the city are in conflict. In fact the city and the group had a major disagreement about the route of the first trail they built together, in 1989. The city attempted to sell one short segment of the corridor that ran through downtown, and proposed an alternate route to bring users around the missing piece. "The parks department had spent all its money on acquisition of the right of way," explains Hammer, "and they were looking to get some money back. I sympathized with their situation, but it was an unacceptable alternative." GPTN members felt the detour proposed by the city was roundabout and lacked proper street crossings. In addition, they felt trail users would simply ignore the spur and take the direct approach anyway. Hammer and her colleagues launched their first public awareness campaign, lobbying newspapers for editorials supporting the more direct, original route. The city council reversed its position.

The GPTN purposefully has avoided obtaining nonprofit status so that it can preserve its right to actively lobby political bodies on trail issues and endorse trail supportive candidates. In order to facilitate its fundraising activities and preserve tax-deductible status for donors, the group has an arrangement with the Nebraska Trails Foundation that allows it to receive contributions for trail acquisition and development.

A quieter kind of advocacy is done by gathering and distributing information. The GPTN conducts an annual census of trail users to find out who is using the trail, and how. Groups of volunteers, located at 8-10 locations on the trail system, collect information over a 14-hour period. The Parks and Recreation Department uses the information for budget purposes as well as to find out about safety issues, such as which trails are more heavily used and at what times of the day, and the numbers of bicyclists and skaters who wear helmets. The information also is made available to the local newspaper and the Lower Platte South Natural Resource District that has responsibility for maintenance of trails outside the city.

Perhaps the best evidence of the group's success is the pervasiveness of the idea that the trails have benefited Lincoln's communities. Developers are building trails actively in new sites and looking to locate new developments near or on existing trails. Although there are continuing difficulties acquiring and building trails within Lincoln's older, densely populated neighborhoods and downtown, realtors advertise prime sites as being located on well-used trails, and transportation officials actively seek to relocate and rebuild trails off of main roads-understanding that the trails are much needed and loved, but can be a hazard when they are narrow bike lanes running alongside highways. This represents a major culture change within the city establishment of which Hammer and the Network are particularly proud.

Name of Park: Lincoln Area Trail System

Location: Lancaster County (Lincoln) Nebraska
Park size: 75 miles

Primary Caretaker: City of Lincoln (within city limits) and Lower Platte South Natural Resource District (outside of city).

Name of Organization: Great Plains Trail Network

Type of Organization: Assistance provider and public advocate

Year Founded: 1989

Staff: None

Board: Maximum of 29 members

Mission: The Great Plains Trail Network is a nonprofit organization that advocates and supports a network of trails in Lancaster County and throughout the State of Nebraska. The network supports a master plan for trails adopted by public officials, seeks financial support through public and private sources, and provides opportunities for persons to use and learn about existing trails.

Master Plan: 1989.

Written Agreements: MOU

Contact:
Elaine Hammer
Great Plains Trail Network
5000 North 7th
Lincoln, NE 68521
(402) 483-2653

www.bikeped.com/gptn

Knox Greenways Coalition

Knox Greenways Coalition

Knoxville, Tennessee

Established in 1991, the Knox Greenways Coalition was formed by a group of three conservationists active in the Sierra Club who believed a greenway system would improve the quality of life and provide recreational opportunities and access to alternative transportation in Knoxville. Will Skelton, a local real estate lawyer, had been inspired by the greenways he had seen throughout his travels in the U.S., Canada and Europe in the 1980's and wanted to continue to develop the existing 1.5-mile greenway that had been started in Knoxville in the 1970's. In the early eighties, Skelton teamed up with Judith Ideker, a landscape architect, and Sam Rogers, another Sierra Club member interested in greenways and water quality, to form the Knox Greenways Coalition. The team created a slide show and brochure and went to speak to local businesses, civic, and conservation groups to build support for a greenway system, promote membership in the coalition, and gather political clout.

Membership grew and, with the coalition's backing, Skelton contacted the mayor and city council members to advocate for the greenway system, resulting in the creation of the Mayor's Greenways Advisory Commission in 1992. The commission was set up to be an official body to plan and implement work on developing the greenways. Skelton was asked to chair the effort and, with him at the helm, the commission undertook the work of creating a greenways plan for the city and county. Approved by the Metropolitan Planning Commission and the city council in 1993, the plan has been broadly publicized since then through television and radio.

Developing the plan for the regional greenway system was not controversial. The mayor's commission, which was made up of representatives from a wide range of constituencies, received input from the city and county, members of the coalition, and citizens through a series of city-wide public hearings. After the plan was created, the city and county established greenways coordinators to implement the plan.

The new Will Skelton Greenway was named after the founder of the Knox Greenways Coalition.

Smokey Mountain Regional Greenway System | Knoxville, Tennessee

RUNNING OVER 20 miles through the city of Knoxville and Knox County, Tennessee are over a dozen greenways, part of a much more substantial regional system that will eventually incorporate the nine contiguous counties around Knoxville.

The current system includes greenways, city parks, trails, and small pocket parks. In some areas, a greenway is adjacent to the Tennessee River, while other greenways are on flood plains. The main arteries of the trail system are planned along three creeks that run through the inner city. When completed, the trail system will contain bike trails and walking paths linking up existing parks in Knoxville and will be accessible to residents in all areas of the city and county. Downtown Knoxville will be the hub of the city-county trail system that someday will connect to the Smoky Mountains National Park, and to the surrounding cities of Oak Ridge, Maryville, Alcoa, Pigeon Forge, Sevierville, and Gatlinburg. So far, sections of the trail have been built in high, middle and low income areas with an emphasis on an equal distribution in all neighborhoods.

The success of the commission was a watershed for the coalition. According to Charles Thomas, president of the coalition, the group considered disbanding after the formation of the mayor's commission, but the members decided that an "outside" force to represent the neighborhoods and lobby the city would be beneficial. With the greenway system being built, the role of the Knox Greenways Coalition shifted to providing political pressure and to lobbying for additional public financial support for the ongoing development and implementation of the greenway.

The coalition now meets only quarterly, and its primary activities consist of advocating for public funds for the greenway system's continued development; advising on greenway design, planning and policy; organizing neighborhood groups to help them develop plans for greenway segments; advocating for continued political support; marketing and outreach to community and politicians; and organizing volunteers. The coalition and the city and county greenway coordinators are all actively involved in organizing communities to participate in the planning and design of the greenway segments as they are developed. To this end, the coalition considers itself a liaison between the city and Knoxville's well-organized neighborhood groups, many of which are now calling for green-

ways in their neighborhoods. These organizations frequently approach the coalition to advise them on the best path to take to influence the city.

The first greenway segment was slated to go through a city park and private property. Community residents were apprehensive about who would use the new greenway and what kinds of activities would develop on and near it. Skelton spent the summer meeting with community groups in the area to resolve their issues and get their support. Working with the community groups paid off. "Now those communities are among the most supportive of the greenway," says Skelton. Other early segments of the greenway system were developed along the city's waterfront and west section in highly visible and populated areas as a way to build support and "spread the word" of the new greenways. Additional greenway segments are being built as land becomes available with the goal to construct one or more miles of greenway in all parts of the city.

According to Skelton, the biggest struggle was over the issue of preserving the trees. "There was a mild dispute with preservationists over how many trees to cut down to make way for the greenway," he related. "The width of the greenway had to be sufficient to ensure that the asphalt wouldn't buckle. Commission members ended up walking the

Strollers on a town of Knoxville Greenway.

trail with the mayor and deciding tree by tree which would stay and which would go."

As a result of the strong support and interest in the greenway by the mayor, the project has been financed entirely by public funds. Much of the funding for greenways comes from the federal Transportation Equity Act for the 21st Century (TEA-21), which has provided over $1 million to date. The city or county have matched those funds by 20% and contributed substantial additional amounts for greenways not funded by TEA-21. Maintenance funding comes from the city parks and recreation departments. To finance its own operations, the coalition offers memberships and holds an annual 5K race along the greenway that raised around $4,000 in 1999. The Knox Greenways Coalition is not a 501(c)(3) corporation, but is rather a loose association of groups interested in advocating for the development of a greenway system. One reason for this is that to date, all funds for the greenway have been public. However in 1998, the coalition provided $1,000 in seed money to a new land trust that its hopes will

be able to raise private funds and acquire parcels of land that the city and county cannot.

The organization's political clout comes from its success in talking with neighborhood groups, and its close connections with the political establishment in Knoxville. The founder of the coalition is, after all, the chairman of the mayor's commission. In addition, the president of the coalition is a member of the mayor's commission, as is the city greenways coordinator. In this way, the Knox Greenways Coalition can work with the city to establish an agenda that is acceptable to both of them, and approach city council members and the mayor, among others, to advocate for that agenda. According to Donna Young, the city greenways coordinator, the coalition is successful because "they are able to get grassroots and political support to work together to further the expansion of the greenway system."

In addition to its work in city hall, the coalition holds an awards ceremony at the annual Metropolitan Planning Commission Banquet to thank political and neighborhood leaders for their support and effort on behalf of the greenway. Awards are given to elected officials, government employees, and neighborhood activists who have made a significant contribution to the greenway over the last year. Occasionally, the coalition will hold a banquet for others involved in the greenway. For example, in the spring of 2000, the coalition had a barbecue for the greenway maintenance workers and engineers. It also distributes a newsletter, and funds a scholarship program for a seminar on habitat gardening.

The primary focus of the city parks and recreation department is on security, design and capital improvements, capital construction, and routine maintenance. The city is involved to a lesser degree in programming, organizing volunteers, advocacy, and marketing and outreach. Young describes her role as the city's greenways coordinator as "seeing the big picture of the greenway." She has a counterpart greenway coordinator who works for the county. The city and county greenway coordinators are part of the city and county parks and recreation departments.

The Mayor's Greenways Advisory Commission is now made up of an 18-member advisory board that includes the city and county greenway coordinators as well as a coalition member. Skelton has daily conversations with the greenway coordinators in the process of implementing the plan and works with the mayor to help facilitate problems as they arise. A $2.2 million greenway along the Tennessee and French Broad Rivers has been named after him and will open officially in Summer 2000.

Name of Park: Smokey Mountain Regional Greenway System

Location: Knoxville, Tennessee

Park Size: 12.8 miles, another 18.1 miles are planned over the next 5 years.

Primary Caretaker: Knoxville City and County Department of Parks and Recreation

Name of Organization: Knox Greenways Coalition

Type: Catalyst

Year Founded: 1991

Staff: None

Mission: "To improve the quality of life in Knoxville and Knox county by the addition of greenways. Greenways provide recreational opportunities (walking biking and in-line skating, jogging, etc.) and alternate transportation routes while protecting water quality along creeks and lakes."

Board: 9 members

Master Plan: 1993

Written Agreements: None

Contact:
Charlie Thomas, President
Knox Greenways Coalition
386 Hiawasse Avenue
Knoxville, TN 37917
(865) 522-7495

The Partnership Organizations

National AIDS Memorial Grove

San Francisco, California

The idea for an AIDS memorial grove in San Francisco was first imagined in 1988 by several members of a city greening organization known as Friends of the Urban Forest, a group of environmentalists who encouraged and helped residents and land owners plant street trees in the city. Two leaders of that organization teamed up with several other local activists to create a natural environment where people could individually and collectively express their grief and concern over the epidemic, which was ravaging communities throughout the San Francisco area. "We all felt the need for a place where people could find solace, solidarity and hope-and the sense of renewal that is inspired by nature," wrote Alice Russell-Shapiro, a founding member of the grove. Originally, the idea was to plant ginko trees in memory of those who had died, but that plan slowly developed into a broader proposal.

The leadership group, at first about five people strong, thought that the best place for their grove would be Golden Gate Park. The park had a good central location in the city, and is well loved by many San Franciscans. They approached the department of Recreation and Parks, which was then under the leadership of Mary Burns. Burns was not discouraging to the group, but she wanted to ensure that the area could be maintained after it was rebuilt. Burns told them that the city would allow them to work in and redesign an area of the park, but that they would have to raise the funds both to do the work and to maintain it.

There were several sections of the park that were in need of repair, including the de Laveaga Dell, which was wildly overgrown and suffered from expensive drainage problems that the city couldn't afford to fix. The group was familiar with the dell, and selected it as the spot for their memorial.

Because the AIDS epidemic had affected a wide spectrum of San Franciscans, and because of

the group's extensive contacts in the environmental movement, the organization was able to gain support, both in-kind and monetary. The first fundraising events were quite successful in gathering the tens of thousands of dollars the group needed to begin building their grove. Nearly everything else was donated. The group met in the basement of one of their founders, Isabel Wade (now the executive director of the San Francisco Neighborhood Parks Council), and relied on a team of prominent architects, landscape architects, and designers who volunteered to create a landscape plan that would serve as a living memorial. The board divided the tasks up to committees and began working.

A spirit of volunteerism quickly caught on among nearly everyone involved with the grove. To launch the operation, the leadership announced a ribbon-cutting ceremony and clean-up day in the dell, and invited the mayor and the press to attend. Their efforts were well received, but more surprisingly they were practically besieged with volunteers, who all chipped in pulling weeds and clearing brush under the guidance of the site committee. This event developed into the most important activity associated with the grove: the monthly workday.

Since 1991, thousands of volunteers have donated their Saturday to the project. "Workdays are the heart of the grove," says Alice Russell-Shapiro. Russell-Shapiro adds that providing people with a way to donate their time and energy to the AIDS cause in a way that is both physically rewarding and spiritually renewing is vital. In addition, others associated with the project added that working in the grove is a way for people without training in health care to help-since most AIDS volunteer work involves direct contact with patients in hospitals and homes. Since working in the grove requires only a willingness to participate, students have used the project as a venue for fulfilling community-service requirements.

National AIDS Memorial Grove | San Francisco, California

IN AN EASTERN section of San Francisco's Golden Gate Park is a shady ravine that shelters the National AIDS Memorial Grove. The seven-acre site, called a "blessed, beautiful sanctuary" by San Francisco Chronicle columnist Ken Garcia13, encloses six flagstone gathering areas, benches, and Sierra granite boulders, some with lines of poetry engraved into them. There are also 17 separate planting areas. The grove's central feature is a large spiral shaped memorial into which are carved the names of hundreds of people who have died of AIDS, or those who wish to be associated with the national memorial. As more names are added, the spiral radiates out further into the clearing. The grove is designed to be a place of reflection, and its many separate spaces allow people to come individually or in groups and find a place of their own. In 1996, the grove was designated the National AIDS Memorial Grove by an act of Congress that was signed into law by President Clinton.

The AIDS Memorial Grove is a small feature of Golden Gate Park, a 1,017-acre green rectangle that runs from the Pacific Ocean through several of San Francisco's most notable neighborhoods, including the neighborhood of Haight-Ashbury, and communities with large Asian, Russian, and African-American populations. The park has long been considered one of the city's prime gathering places. It even housed thousands of homeless after the 1906 fire and earthquake. In the park's original design, the area that is now the AIDS Memorial Grove was a fern garden, known as the de Laveaga Dell. In addition to the grove, the park contains a variety of destinations and institutions, including a large museum, a brew pub, a Japanese Tea Garden, ponds stocked with trout for fly fishing, and a large conservatory.

Over a series of meetings, the board agreed to begin raising funds to endow a gardener to work on the site, to ensure it would be maintained long after the initiative was over, rather than simply raise an annual maintenance budget. "We decided to go with the momentum," said Russell-Shapiro, noting that this approach was a difficult decision, as it required the organization to raise $2 million, instead of over $80,000 annually. However, the establishment of a maintenance endowment and the obvious dedication of the grove's volunteers had a powerful effect on the city, as it allowed the city to view the organization as a long-term partner that would not significantly impact the parks department's bottom-line costs.

The National AIDS Memorial Grove uses the 501(c)(3) designation of the Tides Center, a non-profit public benefit corporation. In 1995, a grant agreement was signed between the Tides Center, a third party designated as the fiscal agent and project sponsor for the grove, and the city and county of San Francisco, acting through its Recreation and Parks Commission. The grant agreement arranges for the National AIDS Memorial Grove project, through the Tides Center, to arrange and pay for site improvements and construction.

The agreement that the grove board eventually worked out with the city is notable for many reasons. First, the city gave a 99-year lease to the grove, contingent on the group's ability to raise the endowment to fund the gardener, who would be a city employee. The grove board insisted that the gardener be on site 100% of the time, to prevent the city from stretching their dollar over the entire park, and the city agreed to establish a workplan for the gardener each year with the

PAUL MARGOLIES

A walk in the AIDS Grove is a time for reflection.

PAUL MARGOLIES

Volunteers help plant and maintain the grove on monthly Saturday workdays.

grove board, and to review that workplan annually.

Currently, the city pays for the salary of a full-time gardener to care for the grove. However, once the endowment is raised, the nonprofit will pick up this cost through annual grants that will be given to the Recreation and Park Department to cover the annual salary of a gardener as well as costs for the purpose of maintaining and improving the memorial grove. The agreement is for 99 years after the completion of the site improvements, and is renewable.

While the grove itself is almost entirely built, and the endowment is nearly raised, the endowment is more than three years behind schedule. The board had originally hoped to raise their endowment by 1997, but various factors have contributed to a shrinking of their funding base. "We're not the new kid on the block anymore," says Russell-Shapiro, who notes that as AIDS research and medicine improves the survival chances of those infected, the disease has moved out of center stage in the public's mind, and has also made it harder for the organization to raise funds. In addition, despite the fact that the AIDS Memorial Grove has received a federal designation, the board has long refused to accept government funds of any kind for the project, believing that public money should go towards research and services for AIDS patients. To make the final push towards full endowment, however, the board will likely accept a one-time-only state grant.

This is not the only funding-related sacrifice the board of the AIDS Memorial Grove has made in its 11-year history. In 1995, with the target date looming and the endowment far from complete, the board made the serious decision to begin creating naming opportunities. The idea had been rejected earlier, because the members felt that putting people's names on things was elitist. However, after pursuing several other strategies, including fundraising events in New York and professional development advice, it soon became apparent that allowing donors to give for certain areas of the grove, or to adopt a bench, was the only serious fundraising option. The most successful venture in this regard is clearly the "Circle of Friends." For $1,000, a donor can add a name to the radiating circle of engraved names that form what is now the central feature of the grove. To create further opportunities, the site committee has also divided up the grove into many distinct areas with names of trees and plants, and priced them accordingly. Nearly all the areas have been "adopted" by donors. The park's 15 benches also have been "adopted" at a cost of $15,000 each.

While originally the board had envisioned that the organization would fold after the grove was completed and the endowment was raised, the current board feels that there should be an organizational future after 2000, and recently changed the organization's mission statement to the following: "The National AIDS Memorial Grove serves as a living tribute to all lives touched by AIDS."

Name of Park: National AIDS Memorial Grove in de Laveaga Dell, Golden Gate Park

Location: San Francisco, California

Park Size: 7 acres

Primary Caretaker: San Francisco Department of Parks and Recreation

---

Name of Organization: National AIDS Memorial Grove

Type of Organization: catalyst

Year Founded: 1989

Staff: 4

Board: 15 members

Mission: "The National AIDS Memorial Grove serves as a living tribute to all lives touched by AIDS."

Master Plan: 1991

Written Agreements: 1995 Grant Agreement

Contact
Thom Weyand, Executive Director
National AIDS Memorial Grove
856 Stanyan Street
San Francisco, CA 94117
(415) 750-8345
aidsmemgrv@aol.com

www.aidsmemorial.org

South Suburban Park Foundation

Arapahoe County, Colorado

When the South Platte River flooded its banks in and around Denver in 1965, it was a last desperate gasp for attention from an abused river that for decades had languished as a dumping ground for the Denver metropolitan area. After the flood, a number of efforts to revitalize and contain the river were spearheaded, including the construction of a 10-mile greenway along the South Platte in downtown Denver, along with riverside parks and access points, boat launches, and chutes for kayaks to navigate the river's dams. The South Platte River Greenway, created by one of the first park nonprofits in the country, has had amazing ripple effects in the region; spawning a regional network of trails and greenways connecting outlying counties, six state parks, and two reservoirs with 150 miles of trails.

In Denver's southern suburbs, the flood on the South Platte captured the attention of the U.S. Army Corps of Engineers, who set to task on the river, building a large dam eight miles south of the city, in Littleton, thereby creating the Chatfield Reservoir. The Corps originally proposed a concrete channel to prevent the river from flooding, but residents and local leaders would not stand for a concrete river. After a long struggle they successfully negotiated an unusual alternate plan. In the alternative, the Army applied the funds from the original channelization project toward creating "softer" edges to the river, and toward the acquisition of parcels in the river's remaining floodplain. On this wetland area, the city of Littleton and the South Suburban Metropolitan Recreation and Park District created the 625-acre South Platte Park.

The struggle with the Army Corps of Engineers had brought the county's strengths to the fore: a shared desire for open space and a concern for the look and feel of the area. After the incident with the Army Corps, and through other venues, the South Suburban Metropolitan Recreation and Park District's five elected officials had become aware

that there were local business leaders interested in parks and in the character of the county, and they saw these leaders as a potential private sector extension of their five-member board.

As early as 1979, district officials had the foresight to understand that as their region grew in population, and as the park acreage under their jurisdiction increased, they would need help raising funds to support acquisition and maintenance of open space. Using Denver's South Platte Greenway Foundation as a model, the officials gathered together several key developers, bankers and other leaders from Arapahoe County and gained their consent for the formation of the South Suburban Park Foundation. The foundation was formed, says Dale Flowers, a charter member, "to help the district do things it couldn't do with taxpayer dollars." The local leaders became the organization's board of directors, and the new organization began meeting and discussing projects for which it could provide support. The board looked into senior facilities and planting trees, but accomplished very little. They needed a big idea.

Among planners and greenway enthusiasts in the area, informal conversations about extending the South Platte River Greenway in Denver into Arapahoe County had been going on for years. A group of greenway supporters, egged on by Bill Woodcock, a planner for the district, enlisted the help of Robert Searns, a local consultant and one of the key developers of Denver's Platte River Greenway. Searns and Woodcock made a presentation to the new South Suburban Park Foundation, highlighting the various benefits of an extended greenway linked to Denver's. The idea was strongly reinforced by the successful model of non-profit participation that was taking place in downtown Denver by the South Platte Greenway Foundation. It was further reinforced for the South Suburban Park District by the new park it had built, which would be connected by the proposed greenway to the Platte River Greenway in Denver.

Mary Carter Greenway | Arapahoe County, Colorado

THE MARY CARTER Greenway begins at the Denver City limit, and runs nine miles along the South Platte River straight through Arapahoe County to the Chatfield Dam. Picking up where the Denver Platte River Greenway stops, the Mary Carter Greenway winds through seven towns, the largest of which is Littleton, Colorado. It is part of a much larger 35-mile system administered by the South Suburban Park and Recreation District. Most of the district's other trails run through parks, or near schools, and are therefore both recreation and commuter oriented. The Mary Carter Greenway, by contrast, exists in a corridor 300 to 1,000 feet wide and includes wildlife trails, boat chutes, and rapids that, when the snow runoff begins to accumulate, can become "downright nasty," according to Bill Woodcock, the South Suburban Park District manager of planning and construction.

The greenway is therefore a regional amenity, used for recreation, long bike rides and walks. It is a continuous concrete trail, eight-to-ten feet wide, which accommodates nearly 600,000 users annually, and as a result, can be quite crowded on busy weekends. The greenway is so popular that the district is considering using an upcoming bond act to expand the trail by adding a second, all-weather surface of crushed stone next to the existing concrete. The second surface would be for walking and jogging.

This greenway serves one of the fastest growing regions in the country and the most populous area of Colorado. Arapahoe County is itself one of the most populous counties in the state, and although the population of the South Suburban Park and Recreation District is listed at less than 165,000, in reality the greenway serves millions of people.

Additionally, the greenway presentation was given a huge boost by the Army Corps of Engineers project on the South Platte that was dredging and channeling the river down to the Chatfield Dam. This project had a little-known "recreation component" that would provide over one million dollars to rehabilitate or build parks and provide access to the newly channeled river if the district could match it. Woodcock wanted to go after the money. "The greenway was a natural fit," said Dale Flowers, the foundation board's chair.

But good ideas need more than their own persuasive force, and the board needed to find financial backing and leadership. The first solid funds arrived in 1982, in the form of a $125,000 challenge grant from the Gates Family Foundation. With the Army Corps money still out of sight, the Gates grant represented the key catalyzing force for the group, noted Searns, who was quickly conscripted into the effort. The following year, the group got the leader they needed when they appointed Mary Carter, then mayor of the town of Bow Mar, Colorado, as chair of the South Suburban Park Foundation.

A charismatic and persuasive politician, Carter went from town to town within the district asking for money to build what was now being called the Arapahoe Greenway. "We kept the vision simple," says Searns, who had been hired by the Foundation as its development consultant and only paid staff member. "We never had a master plan. The greenway at first was just a magic marker line on a piece of paper, running north to south along the length of Arapahoe County." According to Searns, this flexible vision allowed each town to easily "connect the dots" and see the power of the greenway vision as it linked each town to the larger region.

With a tremendous amount of focus, Carter began to pull the jurisdictions together, pool their money, and fund the district's effort to build the greenway mile-by-mile. Once the first mile was completed in 1984, a slide show was put together,

A family takes a ride on the Mary Carter Greenway.

and Carter set out again to raise funds for the next segment. If the magic marker line wasn't enough, Carter took town officials on a tour of Denver's South Platte Greenway. When they saw kayakers and bicyclists and even swimmers on the South Platte River, previously a polluted eyesore, they usually were convinced.

This critical function of bringing partners to the table and broadcasting a vision of the greenway has emerged as the foundation's key role. With Searns as its main consultant (the board is volunteer and there is no paid administrative help) there is also a certain amount of design help and consultation that takes place, but the district contracts for the construction work, builds the greenway, and maintains it. It counts on the foundation solely to provide funds and political support, although the foundation can and occasionally does do a lot more.

For example, by 1989, the dots on Searns' greenway map were connected, and the original trail was close to completion. Ironically, it was at this point that the Army Corps of Engineers money finally became available. The foundation began to consider how it could broaden participation in the trail and begin to establish stewardship among local residents.

The board brainstormed program ideas and other ways of involving residents. Looking at the newly channeled river and greenway, there was a key element missing: trees. The Army had removed many to do its work, and the foundation had sacrificed a few to their cause as well. The foundation decided to promote a huge tree-planting initiative, partnering with a statewide organization called Volunteers for Outdoor Colorado (who would provide the volunteers) and a bank that sponsored the event, and took the concept out to its branches both to encourage local support and additional volunteers for the initiative.

The idea was to plant 10,000 trees. The project took three years to reach its goal, and won several awards in the process. The first year, 1,400 volunteers planted over 2,600 trees and shrubs on 22 acres in one day. The success of the tree planting encouraged the foundation to pursue other large volunteer projects. In 1993, once the 10,000 trees had been planted and the trail was completed, the foundation worked with a grant from Lockheed Martin to build an interpretive center on a spot where three different greenways converged. Over 1,300 volunteers helped build the Discovery Pavilion, which has exhibits and trail information. The Audubon Society has now taken over management of that facility and has plans to expand the site.

The South Suburban Park Foundation has now reached a watershed in its development. Like many non-profit organizations, a certain amount of soul searching has taken place because of a change in leadership. Up until the mid-nineties, the organization focused exclusively on the greenway. Discussions with the district are centering on how the foundation can help with fundraising and development of other park projects, while it continues to build tributary trails and plant along the greenway, now renamed after its late founding chairman, Mary Carter.

The foundation now is helping the district build a water playground. However, it is generally acknowledged among the partners that the foundation board is most enthusiastic about greenways and trails, and less so about projects that broaden the scope of the foundation away from its traditional activities.

Name of Park: Mary Carter Greenway

Location: Denver, CO

Size: 9 miles

Primary Caretaker: South Suburban Park and Recreation District

---

Name of Organization: South Suburban Park Foundation

Type of Organization: Catalyst

Year Founded: 1979

Staff: None

Board: 10 members. Ex-officio member is the manager of planning for the district.

Mission: "To improve the quality of life by helping to fund and develop park, recreation and outdoor improvements in the South Metro Area. To create a legacy of greenways, trails and open space in the South Metro Denver area."

Master Plan: None. However the district has a strategic plan for its entire system of which the greenway is a part.

Partnership Agreements: None

Endowment: None

Contact:
Robert Searns
Urban Edges
8 White Fir Court
Littleton, Colorado 80127
303.904.9415
green49@aol.com

Central Park Conservancy

New York, New York

Management has always been a decisive issue for Central Park. Upon the park's completion, Frederick Law Olmsted wrote, "So far as my judgment or wishes are entitled to any respect in the management of the Central Park this will be regarded as the most critical and important work remaining. The value receivable for all that has hitherto been expended depends upon the skill with which it is done."[15] He would have been pleased to hear that, in the 1940's, though it had undergone many changes, the park was described as being "more carefully tended than at any other time in its history."[14] However, in the 1970s, during the city's dramatic fiscal crisis, Central Park experienced a period of serious neglect, during which time the park's elegant fountains were turned off, its lawns allowed to turn to dust, and Calvert Vaux's stone bridges languished as graffiti-covered eyesores. The park was infamous for illicit activity, and residents feared its under-populated pathways.

PROJECT FOR PUBLIC SPACES

Bethesda Terrace is a key destination in Central Park.

The Department of Parks and Recreation was anxious to improve the park, and in 1973 it attempted a large master planning effort to restore it, but the city's budget was so bereft of funds that the plan was scrapped. By the late seventies, the maintenance of facilities in the park had deteriorated so badly that New York Senator Daniel Patrick Moynihan publicly called the park's condition "a disgrace," and proposed turning it over to the National Park Service.

Throughout this troubled period, several citizen groups united to establish the Central Park Task Force, an organization that began to encourage the direct involvement of the public as park volunteers and donors. In 1979, the group incorporated itself as the Central Park Conservancy, and Elizabeth Barlow Rogers, the head of the Central Park Task Force and the author of a biography of Olmsted, assumed the presidency.

Concurrently, then-Commissioner of Parks Gordon J. Davis was approached with the idea of appointing someone to run the park, in the belief that a centralization of power would address long-term park planning and facilitate fundraising efforts. With a good measure of strategic calculation, Commissioner Davis appointed Rogers the first Central Park Administrator. Though Davis gave Rogers no budget to fund her position or any additional staff, he did give her the authority to make changes. Additionally, in a show of support, Davis launched the first major capital restoration project in the park in years-to restore the 22-acre Sheep Meadow.

Thus the Central Park Conservancy became an organization with one foot in the private sector and one in the public. With limited funds but a broad portfolio, the conservancy set out to change the culture of the parks department and the perception of the park among politicians and city residents. It focused first on raising the standard of park maintenance. Tim Marshall, who was Rogers' deputy administrator and vice president for capital projects and operations, notes that the park employees were working with poor equipment and little support. "They had their hands full just emptying trash cans and cleaning up broken

[14] Letter to C Ryan, Feb. 27th, 1872. The Papers of Frederick Law Olmsted, Vol. IV p. 523.

[15] WPA Guide to New York City, The New Press, 1939; p. 351.

Central Park | New York, New York

CENTRAL PARK DRAWS more than 20 million visits a year, and is one of New York City's most popular attractions. The first large city park in the United States, Central Park was designed by Frederick Law Olmsted and Calvert Vaux in 1858.

Since its inception, the park's much-imitated design has accommodated a variety of activities for New Yorkers. The park's sunken transverses have allowed carriages, and now cars, to cross the park unobtrusively. The Mall, a wide, tree-lined promenade, is a formal arcade, designed for stately strolls. In contrast, the heavily wooded Ramble creates a feeling of dense forest and seclusion. Open meadows give one a sense of natural expanse and have accommodated a few of the largest outdoor concerts in the country, including a Paul Simon concert that drew an estimated 600,000 fans in 1991. The park also plays host to 275 species of birds and sponsors a large group of avid birders. Occupying a prominent place in the iconography of New York, Central Park is where the New York Marathon ends and where John Lennon is remembered in "Strawberry Fields."

But a list of features and events does little to capture Olmsted and Vaux's inspired achievement. According to Elizabeth Barlow Rogers, who is certainly the park's foremost authority, "He [Olmsted] arranged sequences of visual events to climax in stunning vistas...Though every inch of Central Park was shaped and molded by machines and men, the hand of man is never obvious."[16] Indeed, though it seems entirely natural, this 843-acre park is a manmade landscape that cost $14 million to build, and by 1873 had a collection of more than four million trees, shrubs, and plants, a monumental effort, particularly when one considers that New York's largest park at the time was the ten-acre Battery.

In 1937, the city unveiled the park's 15-acre Great Lawn, built over the original site of the Croton Reservoir. Numerous ballfields and playgrounds also have been added to the original design. The park contains many institutions and facilities, including the Metropolitan Museum of Art, several historic buildings and monuments, an outdoor theater, a children's zoo, a science center, a skating rink, and four community centers.

Central Park forms a border for several neighborhoods, extending from some of the city's wealthiest to some of its poorest. Surrounding the southern portions of the park are primarily high-income, high rise apartment buildings, with low to middle income housing near the northern end in Harlem; there is a collection of museums along Fifth Avenue, which forms the park's eastern border.

glass," he added. So the conservancy's first emphasis was on re-establishing the maintenance skills that had been lost from years of mismanagement and budget cuts. This strategy turned into a wholesale emphasis on upkeep and proper maintenance. For example, in the old system, says Marshall, anti-graffiti teams removed the graffiti from the statue of Christopher Columbus once a year, probably right before Columbus Day. "The kids would just wait in the wings to tag it again." Marshall was in charge of initiating a new, stricter policy. In the new system, graffiti had to be removed within 48 hours. Marshall found that once the battle was waged and won on a few fronts, parks employees upped the deadline themselves to 24 hours.

16 Rogers, Elizabeth Barlow, Rebuilding Central Park, a Management and Restoration Plan, MIT Press, 1987, p. 11.

The Central Park Conservancy restored the Harlem Meer in an effort to attract people to the park's North end, and provide better park services for the Harlem community.

According to Marshall, who is now a private consultant, reestablishing the primacy of maintenance in Central Park required instituting training programs and new management structures that would allow the maintenance workers to recognize that they were instrumental in ensuring the health of the park. "Raising the level of commitment, developing a sense of ownership, and new standards of care by the people who are responsible for the day-to-day care of the parks was essential," he added.

Managing and maintaining the park was a huge task, but Rogers had another role for herself in mind. "I had to make the people of New York City see the park in the same light as the Museum of Natural History, or the Bronx Zoo, or the Botanical Gardens," she said, adding, "I wanted them to see it as a major cultural institution, with the trees and lawns as our collection.[17]" To achieve this, the conservancy had to do more than show how beautiful the park could become. They also had to demonstrate that the park was a precious institution in New York that could benefit every sector of the city.

Getting support from the city's large corporations was vital, and Rogers made it a priority to have a board chairman who was a CEO and could reach out to other CEOs. Much of New York's prime residential real estate is focused around the park, due in no small part to the magnitude of Olmsted's vision. This simple fact has allowed the conservancy to reach hundreds of very wealthy donors. The conservancy's largest fundraising event, an annual luncheon hosted by the women's committee in the park's Conservatory Garden, raised $2 million in 1998.

Like many organizations, the conservancy originally limited itself to the design of capital projects, because it couldn't afford to actually make the renovations. A master plan, though not formally adopted by the city, nevertheless became the blueprint for projects in the park. As the organization grew in budget and political clout, the conservancy began funding major capital improvement projects itself, and now provides two-thirds of the park's $22 million operating budget, accounting for most of its gardeners and horticulturalists, as well as staffing the park's programs and visitors centers.

By 1995, after fifteen years of leadership under Rogers, the conservancy had raised more than $110 million to restore and reclaim the park from its nadir in the 1970's. During that time, Rogers developed the conservancy into a premier fundraising and support organization, expanding exponentially from three to 175 employees. In October, 1995, Rogers resigned as conservancy president and park administrator. To take her place, the conservancy board appointed Karen Putnam, the conservancy's vice president for development. In turn, the city appointed Putnam administrator. Since then, this arrangement has changed. Now, the conservancy's senior vice-president for operations and capital projects, not the president works for the city as the Central Park administrator.

---

[17] "Making Partnership Work: The Central Park Model," Achieving Great Parks, Conference Proceedings 1996. (Urban Parks Institute, 1996), p 40.

Despite its obvious success as a fundraiser, the conservancy has discovered that raising money for the park and raising the image, use, and stewardship of the park among all city residents are different things. Erana Stennett, the conservancy's vice president for government and community relations, said, "We try to articulate the benefit of the park to everyone, from the politicians and business community to the schools and churches," said Stennett. She added that when the conservancy shows how the park can be a benefit, businesses see that a healthy, vibrant park helps attract top executives and companies to Manhattan, or keep them from fleeing, and schools see that their needs for curriculum enhancement can be fulfilled with park programming.

Partnerships with schools, faith-based organizations, neighborhood groups and many others also bring volunteers and users. "The conservancy concept can be replicated," Stennett insists. "It's not just about raising money from the wealthiest New Yorkers. It's about getting buy-in from all the residents, businesses, schools, all the industries that surround the park, and getting them to see that Central Park is a resource for them."

To increase public involvement in the park and the planning process, the conservancy has stepped up outreach and marketing, as well as its commitment to programming. Public advisory committees evaluate conservancy programs, review capital improvements, and recommend new management and restoration strategies. In addition, these groups advise the conservancy on trends and issues of concern to park users. New programs have also broadened audience diversity through collaborations with community groups and neighboring institutions, bringing entirely new audiences to previously underused areas in the park. For example, the fishing derby at the restored Harlem Meer attracts over 2,800 people from New York City's five boroughs, New Jersey, and Westchester County to a section of the park that abuts East Harlem. Until its renovation, many New Yorkers avoided the Meer and its adjacent park building.

In 1998, the New York City Department of Parks and Recreation and the conservancy signed a long-term contract that formalizes their relationship. The agreement allows for the city to contract directly with the conservancy for virtually all of the park's maintenance responsibilities including: cleaning of facilities, playgrounds, drains and walkways; landscape maintenance; repairs and painting (including monuments); and capital improvements, which will continue to undergo review by the parks commissioner and by the public. Under the terms of the agreement, the city pays the conservancy an annual fee based on the amount of money the conservancy raises and spends on the park, and on the amount of income the city generates from concessions in the park.

Name of Park: Central Park

Location: New York City, NY

Park Size: 810 acres

Primary Caretaker: Central Park Conservancy

Name of Organization: Central Park Conservancy

Type of Organization: Co-manager

Year Founded: 1980

Staff: 216

Board: 52 members. 43 trustees Ex-Officio: DPR Commissioner, Manhattan Borough President, Central Park Administrator, the President of the Women's Committee of the Conservancy; 5 Mayoral appointees.

Mission: "To restore, manage, and protect Central Park and to educate and serve its users and patrons."

Master Plan: 1987

Written Agreements: City contract, 1997

Contact:
Erana Stennett
Vice President for Government and Community Relations
Central Park Conservancy
14 East 60th Street, 8th Floor
New York, NY 10022
(212) 310-6660
estennet@centralparknyc.org

www.centralparknyc.org

Forest Park Forever

St. Louis, Missouri

Dirt is flying in St. Louis' Forest Park, as craftsmen restore its historic buildings, volunteers and horticulturists plant tens of thousands of trees and other flora, and engineers reestablish a river's natural course in an astonishingly bold $86 million restoration project. The project, jointly funded by the city of St. Louis and private sector donations, is the result of a hard-won consensus master plan among the residents of St. Louis, the city government, and many cultural institutions that inhabit the park. Forest Park Forever, a nonprofit organization that has raised most of the private funds to restore the park, is helping to facilitate the park's revitalization along with the St. Louis Department of Parks, Recreation and Forestry.

The long process began in the late 1970's, when the mayor of St. Louis and the director of the Department of Parks, Recreation and Forestry became concerned about the deteriorating conditions in Forest Park and hired a consultant team to develop a master plan. The planning process, which involved extensive public outreach at the time, was completed in 1981, but approval of the master plan was interrupted by a mayoral race and did not occur until 1983.

The Forest Park master plan included recommendations for the creation of a park manager/administrator position in the city government, as well as the formation of a private partner to help raise additional money for improvements. The approved plan did not include a landscaping scheme, the thought being that a plan would be prepared as part of a next stage for detailing necessary park restoration improvements.

In 1985, Nancy Rice, the director of Parks, Recreation and Forestry, created the position of Forest Park Manager within her department with the task of developing a nonprofit entity and managing its relation with the city. At the same time, Mary Stolar, an attorney, former alderman, and park advocate with strong connections to the constituencies surrounding the park, approached Rice about getting involved. Rice hired her as the first manager of Forest Park.

As Forest Park Manager, Stolar enlisted the help of Evelyn Newman, a well-known neighborhood resident with fundraising experience to chair and bring together members of the new nonprofit's first board of directors. With an official announcement of their role by the mayor to spur them on, the two set to work and in 1986, Forest Park Forever was founded to work with the city toward "making Forest Park the premier park in the United States." Stolar served as the executive director. Once a board of directors was in place, the nascent organization developed by-laws and applied for 501(c)(3) status with help from the parks department. Stolar and the board president went to talk with Betsy Barlow Rogers at the Central Park Conservancy to see what they could learn from her that could be applied to Forest Park.

However, an audit conducted by the state of Missouri in 1989 flagged the dual role of the Forest Park Manager and Forest Park Forever executive director as a violation of a state law preventing the use of private funds for public projects. As a result, the city split up the position. The park manager, a city employee, would be responsible for day-to-day operations and maintenance of the park, and liaison activities to the cultural institutions in the park. The director of Forest Park Forever became primarily concerned with fundraising and capital improvements.

Initial fundraising campaigns launched by the fledgling nonprofit focused on renovating existing facilities. For example, the park's famous King St. Louis statue was restored, the Victorian Bridge was repaired, new benches and picnic pavilions were installed, and "Turtle Park," a children's playground featuring huge sculptured turtles, was designed and installed by artist Bob Cassilly. Several of these projects, funded solely by private donations, were managed entirely by Forest Park

Forest Park | St. Louis, Missouri

ONE OF THE largest urban parks in the country, Forest Park consists of more than 1,290 acres of turf, woodlands, wetlands, and water. Designed by Maximilian Kern and built in 1876, the park originally had a much more wild and natural feel than it does today. The transition is due in part to the 1904 Louisiana Purchase Exposition, a World's Fair held in Forest Park, which necessitated the building of cultural and recreational structures, and had the end result of encouraging more active uses.

Later in the century, interstate highways were built flanking the park, claiming more than 80 of its original 1,370 acres. The St. Louis Zoo, Missouri History Museum, St. Louis Art Museum, St. Louis Science Center, the Muny Theater, 36 holes of golf, a conservatory, an ice skating rink, and a boathouse are all located in the park. These institutions and modifications have made the park more accessible for St. Louisians and provided them with many activities, and, as a result, Forest Park now attracts over 12 million visitors annually. However, such intensive use has dramatically altered the park's character, and it is now being rebuilt in the hope that it can better serve contemporary uses while better reflecting its original design.

Due to its strong associations with the 1904 Exposition, which represented the city at perhaps its apex of influence, the park inspires St. Louisians, and is close to their hearts. Recently, an editorial in the St. Louis Post-Dispatch declared, "Forest Park is a symbol of the city at its finest hour, a green and grassy reminder of the World's Fair and a time when St. Louis' sense of its own destiny was as grand as that of any city in the country."[18] As a regional park, Forest Park serves a metropolitan population of 2.5 million people. As a city park, it serves the institutions and 400,000 residents who live within its five-mile radius, and area that includes the BJC Medical Complex (the city's largest employer), Washington University, low and moderate-income residential areas, and neighborhoods of historic homes. The park is the site of two major citywide celebrations, the St. Louis Kite Festival and the Great Forest Park Balloon Race.

Forever, which paid for the design costs, contracted and oversaw the construction, and continues to pay for the maintenance of these various facilities.

In 1989, Forest Park Forever commissioned the firm of Kelly-Varnel to study park conditions and to develop a landscape plan for the park. This effort turned into a full revision of the 1983 master plan. When the completed document was sent to the city for review and approval in the midst of an election year, the plan fell by the wayside.

However, capital improvements were a priority of the newly elected mayor, and one of his first acts in office was to facilitate the passage of a long

attempted state legislative bill that allocated a half-cent portion of the state's sales tax to the city for capital improvements. Passed in 1993, the mayor allocated 17% of the generated revenue from the state sales tax for capital improvements in the city's parks. Forest Park received $1.9 million the first year.

Concurrent with the mayor's activities, the city decided that a fresh start was needed for Forest Park and its plan. Instead of hiring an outside con-

18 October 5, 1998; editorial, St. Louis Post-Dispatch, "Growing New Leadership," p B1.

sultant, the Department of Parks, Recreation and Forestry used the new funds to lead a highly inclusive public master planning process for the park by itself. According to Forest Park Manager Anabeth Calkins, the city began to build community support for the master plan in 1992, formally launching the city-led community design and development process with a summit in December 1993. The final document declared that the master plan was instituted "based on the notion that the design [of the park] and the design process itself should be the mechanism for conflict resolution, public education, empowerment of the stakeholders and citizens, and the recognition by the public of what constitutes design excellence." Armed with the dedicated source of $1.9 million from the new state sales tax, the master planning process for Forest Park gained momentum, generating greater confidence among the public as well as from the philanthropic community that the plan would be implemented.

The two-year master planning process involved considerable public input through a summit meeting, interviews with community representatives, and a series of public meetings and forums. The final Forest Park Master Plan was produced and ultimately approved by the city in 1995. Forest Park Forever's third executive director, Sue Clancy, hired in 1993, participated in the city's master planning process both as part of the oversight and final decision-making executive committee appointed by the mayor, and as one of the 69-member Forest Park Master Plan Committee.

The approved Forest Park Master Plan has served as a foundation upon which the partnership between Forest Park Forever and the parks department is built. "By clearly identifying specific capital improvement goals, the master plan has provided a clear agenda for both public and private partners," says Jim Mann, Forest Park Forever's fourth and current executive director. The development of the master plan has brought other benefits as well. The plan has inspired a capital campaign for the park of breathtaking

There is an agreement between the parties that all projects will be financed equally with private and public money.

proportions—$86 million is the target sum, and the nonprofit will split this effort with the city, which has pledged its $43 million.

In the four years since the approval of the plan, Forest Park Forever has raised $37 million in payments and pledges. In 1999 alone, it received nearly $10 million in contributions towards the capital campaign. Additionally, the Forest Park Trust, a private maintenance endowment, currently has $3,200,000 in funds. (For a discussion of Forest Park Forever's extensive fundraising plan, see Chapter 3.) Anabeth Calkins credits "the groundwork of enormous community support laid during the process of developing the master plan" as an important reason why the fundraising efforts for Forest Park have been so successful. Completion of the capital projects identified in the master plan is targeted for the anniversary of the World's Fair in 2004.

Fundraising, however, is only half the struggle, as Forest Park Forever and the parks department have begun the massive effort of actually renovating the park's facilities based on the recommendations of the master plan. There is an agreement between the parties that all projects will be financed equally with private and public money. Once the design of a project is approved, Forest Park Forever transfers its portion of the funds into a holding company, and the city issues the construction contracts.

The partnership is in the process of repaving the park's roads and closing others, which is never an easy task. A new lighting program has been put into place, the intent of which is to replace the park's ubiquitous "cobra head" lights with fixtures that are more sensitive to the historic character of the park. Another project just underway is the construction of a second path next to the park's extremely popular paved bike path. This, along with the road closings, should go a long way toward reducing conflicts between bikes, cars, skaters, and runners.

But these projects pale in comparison to the river and wetlands restoration program underway.

This project attempts to re-create the effect that the River Des Peres had on the park. The river, which originally flowed through Forest Park, was completely covered up for the World's Fair. Regular flooding in the areas where the river used to be has plagued Forest Park for nearly a century. The master plan's solution to the floods was to bring the river back. Though the original river will remain channelized underground, a new river is being dredged along the general route the old one took through the park. This massive project, currently flirting with a $20 million price tag, has involved a complete overhaul of the park's sewer and drainage systems, the relocation of a parking lot, the construction of several bridges, and the planting of thousands of new plants and trees. The new waterway system will eventually connect most of the park's water bodies to one another, dramatically improve the water quality in the park (because water will now circulate instead of lying stagnant in pools), and create wetland environ-

ments that the city and the organization hope will attract wildlife. Moreover, these wetlands will be significantly easier to maintain than the current mowed fields that are frequently wet and often in need of repair as a result.

Other capital projects include a new boathouse and golf clubhouse, the restoration of several structures such as the Art Deco "Jewel Box" plant conservatory, and a reconfiguration of 27 holes of golf.

Further demonstrating its intention to actively offer support, the city of St. Louis has issued $17 million of Forest Park Improvement Bonds, to be repaid through the city sales tax. This money is currently going directly into the park. Once the bond has been repaid, in approximately 25 years, the revenue from the same city sales tax will be directed towards the park. In addition, the Missouri Department of Natural Resources has contributed $1.2 million towards needed improvements on the park's waterway systems.

Building Turtle Park was an early project for Forest Park Forever.

However, the 50/50 joint-funding arrangement between the city and Forest Park Forever is not perfect, and it is currently under renegotiation. One major problem relates to timing. The city bureaucracy moves quite a bit slower than the nonprofit would like when arranging for a new project. As a result, Forest Park Forever is actually raising money quite a bit faster than the city can spend it, and in some cases has raised the entire amount necessary to fund certain improvements. The organization would like to be able to move ahead on these projects with city approval. "In projects where we raise all the cash, we want to be more involved," said Jim Mann. Occasionally, to speed a project along, the nonprofit has paid for an architect to design an improvement by itself, and sent that through the city approval process, instead of waiting for the city to go through its normal design process. This process is risky, because the city could reject the design, but, says Mann, "If a donor pays for a project, the donor ought to be able to see and approve

the design before it is constructed." Since the completion of the new master plan, one major project—the $1.1 million renovation of the World's Fair Pavilion—has been financed and built entirely with private funds.

The nonprofit also has spearheaded the development of a new maintenance plan for the park. The plan recommends the establishment of a dedicated maintenance staff that would work exclusively in Forest Park. Increased staff levels for park maintenance would be funded by the nonprofit. The plan also recommends a zone maintenance strategy, much like the one currently in place in New York City's Central Park (see Chapter 3, Sec. 7, Routine Maintenance).

With several grants from national foundations, Forest Park Forever has also launched a program that brings schoolchildren into the park on a regular basis to learn about the environment through a mobile ecology classroom known as the "EcoLab." The lab also is used during events, such as a recent

The Jewel Box, Forest Park.

Earth Day celebration. The organization also has developed informational materials and maps, and manages several volunteer programs for members to participate in plantings, clean-ups, and events. Forest Park Forever has also developed a series of brochures on wildlife and plants in the park to increase awareness and stewardship among park users.

Name of Park: Forest Park

Location: St. Louis, Missouri

Size: 1290 acres

Primary Caretaker: Parks Division, Department of Parks, Recreation and Forestry

---

Name of Organization: Forest Park Forever

Type: Co-manager

Year Formed: 1986

Mission: The mission of Forest Park Forever is to make Forest Park the premier urban park in the country.

Staff: 6

Board Composition: 60. Ex-Officio members include the Forest Park Manager and the heads of the cultural institutions within the park.

Master Plan: 1995, completion date is 2004

Written Agreements: 1997 MOU with city of St. Louis (1997-2004)

Contact:
Jim Mann, Executive Director
Forest Park Forever
5595 Grand Drive in Forest Park
St. Louis, MO 63112
314/367-7275
jmann@forestparkforever.org

www.forestparkforever.org

Friends of Hermann Park

Houston, Texas

The Friends of Hermann Park was founded in 1991 by a small group of influential Houston residents who lived in a condominium overlooking one of the park's major features - the reflection pool. Originally calling themselves the Neighbors of Hermann Park, their group expanded quickly as their interest in improving the park caught on. Less than a year later, the neighbors renamed themselves the Friends of Hermann Park and began raising funds to restore a fountain and improve lighting on a trail within the park.

In 1992, with considerable support from the city, and in partnership with the Rice University Design Alliance, the friends launched a major design competition for the park's feature elements. The competition asked designers to focus on the "Heart of the Park," which included the main entrance, a reflection pool, and a statue of Sam Houston that together serve as Hermann Park's centerpieces. The national competition brought attention to the needs of the park as a whole, and pointed out to the friends, and to other Houstonians, including the mayor, that the entire park was in need of a major restoration.

Following the design competition, discussions among a conglomerate of numerous park advoca-

Girls enjoy the Old Fashioned Fall Festival in Hermann Park, 1997.

cy organizations and the city about the need for a comprehensive master plan began to bear fruit. It was at this point that the friends-believing that a master plan was the first step to broader interest in revitalizing Hermann Park-hired a full time executive director and a staff assistant. With significant support from Mayor Bob Lanier, the friends raised more than $310,000 to fund the master plan.

The master plan was completed in 1995 by the firm of Hanna/Olin after a lengthy process that involved meetings with community groups and discussions with the various institutions that are located in the park. The plan was adopted by the friends in 1995 and approved by the City Council in 1997. The friends are currently working with the city of Houston Parks and Recreation Department to develop a master plan for the 'maintenance of the park.

The friends are heavily invested in the master plan, which is their guiding document for renovations and projects. Although endorsed by the city, the plan has come under attack from the institutions in the park, most seriously over the issue of parking.

According to Laurie Olin, the master plan's architect, parking along the park's major access road has caused serious traffic congestion and overuse of the park's central area and features, leaving its more remote places neglected. In the plan, parking would be restricted on the main road, and new lots would be added around the perimeter of the park, to encourage people to walk into the center and explore other parts of the park, in addition to easing traffic through the park's core. In addition, Olin suggested that a large parking area in the center of the park be "reclaimed...for public use" by creating what he called "Houston's own Great Lawn." Decentralizing parking and creating a large central lawn was the foundation of Olin's plan, and enthusiastically supported by the friends. However, the new plan was less well received by the park's major

FRIENDS OF HERMANN PARK

Hermann Park | Houston, Texas

HERMANN PARK IS a 446-acre park located in central Houston several miles south of downtown. One of the city's most significant cultural and recreational resources, it serves not only its immediate neighbors but a regional population as well. Over five million people visit the park's attractions every year, which include the Houston Zoological Gardens, the Houston Museum of Natural Science, the Miller Outdoor Theatre, the Japanese Garden, the Houston Garden Center, an 18-hole municipal golf course, a lake, and Brays Bayou. An original scheme for the park was proposed in the early 1900's by George Kessler, whose ideas were broadly drawn upon for a General Plan, developed by the city with the architecture firm of Hare and Hare in the 1920's. However, the plan was significantly amended by Hare and Hare as the city added cultural institutions, sports facilities, an environmental preserve and a limited amount of open space without designated programmatic purposes.

Historically, Hermann Park always has been frequented by the broad spectrum of Houston's very diverse but usually segregated population. Primarily high-income housing surrounds the park, with one side of the park facing a low-to-middle income area. In addition, a university, hotel, hospital, medical center and museum are located within the immediate area and a major roadway runs along one border of the park. The park's nearest neighborhood is the Third Ward. The cultural and educational center of Houston's African-American community, the Third Ward houses both Texas Southern University and the University of Houston. More than 37% of Third Ward residents have incomes ranging from under $10,000 in the north to approximately $20,000 along Brays Bayou. Many Third Ward residents use Hermann Park as their neighborhood park.

institutions—the zoo, museum, and theater—all of which rely heavily on cars and buses to bring customers to their doors.

After many meetings, the friends realized that the parking issue was simply not resolved adequately in the master plan, and to some extent only served to alienate the institutions from the friends. A compromise parking plan, the result of much hard work, is now being implemented, and is based on a parking charette that was conducted in January 2000.

Parking aside, the friends have been able to complete several other noteworthy projects identified in the master plan. They raised funds to support $5.4 million in renovations to the Miller Theater, an expansion and renovation of McGovern Lake, with an aeration system, pier and boathouse for $3.6 million. The friends also oversaw $1.1 million in renovations to the Bayou Parkland, an 80-acre area along Brays Bayou that is extensively programmed by the friends for environmental education, and now includes a multiuse pavilion, new picnic areas, furnishings and forest trails. A $3.5 million renovation of the golf course by a private contractor who runs the facility was completed in September 1999.

As specified by the Memorandum of Understanding, Friends of Hermann Park funds all of the design cost and half of the construction/execution costs of the master plan's capital projects; the city finances the other half of the construction/execution costs.

The staffs of the friends and the Department of Parks frequently work together on capital project plans. Usually, a design team with members from both works together on initial designs for capital projects. Although the construction costs are shared, design costs have typically been borne by the friends. "By having more control over the design phase of capital projects," says Roksan Okan-Vick, president of the friends, "we believe that we have been able to maintain a higher level of quality control over project designs." The group also has initiated most of the design proposals, but as the ultimate authority over the park, the Parks Department can reject project proposals.

In addition to capital projects, the friends are active in special events, fundraising, and programming. They expect to expand their limited involvement in maintenance within the next few years, as the capital projects are completed. To this point, maintenance and security have remained primarily the responsibility of the Houston Department of Parks.

The Friends of Hermann Park is funded primarily through large grants and by wealthy individual donors. An annual luncheon and golf tournament have been especially lucrative fundraisers. The City Council has made a $10.1 million commitment to the group in the form of community improvement bonds towards the realization of the master plan.

Name of Park: Hermann Park

Location: Houston, Texas

Size: 400 acres

Primary Caretaker: Houston Department of Parks and Recreation

---

Name of Organization: Friends of Hermann Park

Type of Organization: Co-manager

Staff: 8

Board: 39 members

Mission: The Friends of Hermann Park, a non-profit citizens organization, is dedicated to the protection and enhancement of one of Houston's most historically significant public green spaces. Its goals are to preserve the integrity of Hermann Park, enrich its heritage as a unique landmark, and transform it into one of the nation's premier urban parks.

Master Plan: Hanna/Olin, 1995

Written Agreements: M.O.U., 1997

Contact
Ms. Roksan Okan-Vick
Executive Director
Friends Of Hermann Park
P.O. Box 541447
Houston, Texas 77254-1447
713-524-5876 / 713-524-5887 fax
fhp@hermannpark.org

www.hermannpark.org

PUBLIC PARKS PRIVATE PARTNERS •

Louisville Olmsted Parks Conservancy

Louisville Olmsted Parks Conservancy
Louisville, Kentucky
Although Louisville has one of the few city park systems designed by Olmsted and his firm, by the 1970's, Louisville's parks had a problem. The parks were mostly unused. This happened for several reasons. First, the Louisville/Jefferson County Department of Parks and Recreation had lost ground radically in the 1940s, when the parks commission was dissolved and its responsibilities were divided up among various city agencies. As a result, there was a complete loss of institutional memory about these historic spaces and why they were originally designed that way. In addition, tornados and floods had destroyed vital pieces of the Olmsted vision, and capital rebuilding projects had in some cases, rendered that vision even more inscrutable.

According to Susan Rademacher, Louisville's assistant parks director for planning and design,

the genesis for the renewal of the city's Olmsted landscapes was in 1986, when the parks department wrote a grant that helped to fund the creation of an advocacy group, the Louisville Friends of Olmsted Parks. The new group's first task was to inventory the 180 properties that had been developed by the Olmsted firm over a period of almost 50 years. In the process, says Rademacher, "they began to see that the parks were truly becoming fragmented, that development was extremely piecemeal, and that the power of the park landscape was being lost, in terms of community opportunities."

The friends sought advice from Elizabeth Barlow Rogers of the Central Park Conservancy, who met with stakeholders and recommended that a separate entity be formed (in addition to the friends) specifically to raise money for the parks, develop a master plan, and undertake capital projects to improve the parks. Since the friends

Designing recreation facilities that are consistent with an Olmsted landscape, like this one in Shawnee Park, is one key role of the Louisville Olmsted Parks Conservancy.

TED WATHEN, QUADRANT

Louisville Olmsted Parks System | Louisville, Kentucky

FREDERICK LAW OLMSTED and his successors worked in Louisville, Kentucky for over 40 years, from 1891-1921. Olmsted and his son conceived of the Louisville system and worked on it together until Olmsted Sr.'s retirement in 1895. Olmsted's sons John Charles and Frederick Law Olmsted, Jr., continued to work actively in Louisville until 1912, occasionally consulting with the city until 1935. Over that time they designed 16 parks and 5 parkways-about 2,000 acres and 15 miles of parkways-around which the whole city-county park system is built.

The heart of the Olmsted scheme is three major regional parks: Iroquois Park is a huge, rugged hill offering spectacular vistas of the surrounding area from its overlooks. Cherokee Park, to the east, is a pastoral setting with Beargrass Creek winding its way among cliffs, woods, and meadows. Designed mostly for scenery and nature, these two parks are in contrast to Shawnee Park, on the western edge of the city. Shawnee Park is a low-lying riverfront park with a sweeping view of the Ohio River. Olmsted designed Shawnee, with its level terrain and more formal approach, for large gatherings and events. These three parks total nearly 1,500 acres of the 9,374-acre park system in the city Louisville.

were not constituted for that purpose, did not have a board with those skills, and preferred to focus on awareness and advocacy, they endorsed Barlow's recommendation.

Former mayor Jerry E. Abramson appointed his own committee to study the issue. Two years later, he came to the same conclusion and encouraged the formation of the Louisville Olmsted Parks Conservancy as a planning and funding partnership between the city and private sector. He allocated $1 million in seed money to establish the conservancy and fund the master plan for Shawnee, Iroquois and Cherokee Parks and parkways. In 1989, the conservancy was incorporated as a nonprofit entity with a board of 33 trustees. To date, the conservancy has raised more than $8 million in donations, to leverage an additional $4.5 million in city investment towards the restoration effort. The friends continue to operate as an advocacy organization with a grassroots orientation.

Like many partnerships, the conservancy's organizational structure has evolved over time. Initially, the parks department agreed that the conservancy's executive director would also have the title of assistant director of parks, and the conservancy footed the bill. But the position is now a

dual one: the president of the conservancy splits her time as assistant director of the parks department in charge of planning and design, with half her salary paid by the conservancy, half by the public sector. She supervises a public staff of nine, including landscape architects, civil engineers, planners, and computer service staff as well as a conservancy staff of six, including development, program, and marketing staff, a business manager, and a project manager. Susan Rademacher was hired to serve in this unique dual position.

Today, the Parks Department has responsibility for maintenance, recreation programs and events. Since the city's funding is limited, the parks department funds basics like infrastructure and operations. The conservancy focuses on improving the park experience, for example by providing a greater variety of recreation opportunities and focusing on improving the character and landscapes in the parks, as well as initiating experimental projects such as wetlands restoration.

Because its role centers on providing planning and design expertise, the conservancy's board felt that a master plan should be completed to ensure the long-term health and maintenance of the Olmsted parks. With city support and funds raised from the board, the conservancy hired Andropogon Associates of Philadelphia to develop a master plan, which recommended $50 million in park improvements. The plan, which involved input from 600 citizens and an analysis of current user needs, and recommended restoring historic open spaces and vistas, refurbishing trails, developing new sports areas and support facilities, and rehabilitating the parks' woodlands and natural systems. The plan emphasized the importance of management and stewardship and envisioned a central role for volunteers and community residents.

Preparation of the master plan involved ecological and historical landscape architects, engineers, historians, parks department maintenance staff, park users, and city council members and took three years to produce. Rademacher calls it "a blending of ecological restoration and historic preservation which I consider to be a real accomplishment." She adds that the community was invited to participate in every phase of the process, but that the best leaders were specifically cultivated to serve as advisors. "Every person who had written a letter to the editor or called in to complain about a park-related issue was invited," she said. "Of this group we eventually found the people who were committed enough to be on the new stewardship councils. The councils met as needed; consulting with the planning team whenever they needed input."

With a solid master plan in place, the conservancy can oversee and review projects put forward by the aldermen and neighborhood associations (the nonprofit also has the right to recommend against projects not based on the master plan, since the aldermen have adopted it as a guiding document), as well as select capital projects in the parks that are developed with the parks department.

As the conservancy began to look at correcting the years of unorganized building and remodeling that had taken the parks far away from their original design and intent, they saw conflicts. Since the needs of users had changed dramatically since the Olmsted firm designed these parks 100 years ago, the conservancy has had to pursue a delicate strat-

Like many partnerships, the conservancy's organizational structure has evolved over time.

egy of restoring Louisville's historic parks, while allowing for the recreational and other needs of the contemporary citizenry. For example, city and park planners had added ballfields and courts in the parks as they saw fit, with little regard to their effect on the overall landscape. "Deteriorated sports facilities were scattered throughout the historic landscape," said Rademacher.

To address these issues, the conservancy raised money for, and is now building, a $3 million recreation complex on parkland added to one of the major Olmsted parks. They are also providing all the other amenities needed for such a facility, such as parking, water fountains, and comfort stations, as well as concentrating on the new facility's potential for other uses, its connections to other parks, neighborhoods and trails in the city, and its aesthetics. "We are trying to think about what ballfields have to look like to be compatible with this landscape," says Rademacher, adding that when the facility isn't in active use, the surrounding landscape should be available for passive recreation. The facility's location, adjacent to the park instead of smack in the middle of it, was also a key consideration.

Rademacher is hopeful that by addressing recreation needs in this way; she can be more faithful to the Olmsted plan without sacrificing the recreation component that the city's residents need and demand. "It is precisely this kind of activity—one which allows for planning and historical renovation—that the conservancy was established to provide for Louisville," she added.

The conservancy, in addition to its fundraising and capital planning and construction, also organizes volunteers for landscaping and other remedial maintenance activities such as Park Champions, a group of volunteers that works for the park in myriad ways. Some volunteers work on trails and landscape maintenance projects in the parks. Others serve on community committees that address park needs, perform clerical tasks, and serve as information resources in the parks. In the future, the conservancy plans to develop and provide training for Parks Department staff in landscape restoration and management techniques, facility maintenance, and greeting and assisting the public. They also are developing a system for tracking maintenance needs in the flagship Olmsted Parks and plan to conduct an annual maintenance review to identify and prioritize needed repairs or management adjustments. To fund this effort, the organization takes 30% of the capital donations to the park from individuals and corporations to supply an endowment. Similar to a maintenance fund, the endowment pays for the review and other organizational tasks.

The conservancy eschews more aggressive advocacy—something it prefers to delegate to the friends, which effectively spearheaded the successful permanent closing of a traffic lane for pedestrian and bicycle use in one of the Olmsted parks. "Basically," says Rademacher, "the Louisville Friends of Olmsted Parks works from the outside advocating for the parks, while the conservancy works from the inside."

Name of park: Louisville Olmsted Park System

Location: Louisville, Kentucky

Size: 15 miles of parkway, 1200 acres of parkland

Primary Caretaker: Metro Parks

Name of Organization: Louisville Olmsted Parks Conservancy

Type: Co-manager

Staff: 6

Board: 42 members. Ex-officio: Director of Public Works, 3 Mayoral representatives, Director of Parks, Parks Advisory Board, Friends of Olmsted Parks.

Mission: "To preserve and enhance Louisville's legacy of Olmsted parks and parkways for generations to come."

Master Plan: 1994, Andropogon Associates

Written Agreements: master grant agreement, master operating agreement

Contact:
Susan Rademacher, President
Louisville Olmsted Parks Conservancy
1297 Trevillan Way
P.O. Box 37280
Louisville, KY 40233
(502) 456-8125
srademacher@louky.org

Piedmont Park Conservancy

Atlanta, Georgia

The history of the Piedmont Park Conservancy, like many nonprofit parks organizations, begins with controversy. In the mid 1980s, a proposed sewer improvement plan was expected to have a significant negative impact on the park. The plan, and the reaction to it, brought intense attention to the declining condition of Piedmont Park. A political power struggle ensued over the control of the restoration of the park. Eventually, a consensus was reached among the Midtown Business Alliance, a local business association, the parks commissioner, and the Friends of Piedmont Park-functioning primarily as a grassroots advocacy group—to create a public—private partnership to improve park conditions.

Led by the friends, research into existing park partnership models was conducted. The group held conversations with Betsy Barlow Rogers, then president of the Central Park Conservancy, and with Tupper Thomas, the president of the Prospect Park Alliance. In 1989, with the support of elected officials, various community organizations, and a $200,000 gift toward organizational operations from a local businessman, the Piedmont Park Conservancy was established as a means to protect the park from negative encroachments and to improve park conditions. The conservancy was an outgrowth of the Friends of Piedmont Park. With the friends already established as a 501(c) (3), the conservancy assumed the friends' nonprofit status.

Today, the conservancy has developed a membership of over 1,000, and raised $12 million in capital funds to restore the park's entrances, landscapes, and historic structures. Operational funds come primarily from fundraising efforts and the rental of park spaces and buildings for private functions.

The conservancy's first years were marked by the need to raise substantial funds for park improvements. The first order of business was to develop a plan that would determine the types of improvements required, and to work out issues of mutual trust and organizational roles with the city of Atlanta.

The conservancy, first housed within the offices of the Midtown Alliance, formalized its partnership with the city in a Memorandum of Understanding (MOU) in 1992. The MOU identified the conservancy as the main vehicle for interested parties to become involved with the park as advocates, volunteers, and donors. The conservancy has since relocated its offices into one of three turn-of-the-century park maintenance buildings, one of the projects for which it raised funds in their original $6.5 million capital campaign. The group is now in the midst of a $15 million fundraising initiative, called "Atlanta's Green Heart," to make improvements to the park landscape, cover operating expenses, and begin an endowment.

From 1993-1995 a master plan was produced, and has become the guiding force behind all decisions and improvements made to the park. A 26-member Master Plan Advisory Committee guided the process, with representatives from professional organizations and citizens selected by the conservancy and city council. A preliminary concept plan was developed and used in five public hearings to

Lake Clara Meer, Piedmont Park.

Piedmont Park | Atlanta, Georgia

PIEDMONT PARK is one of the largest and oldest parks in the metropolitan Atlanta region. First a family farm, and later a Civil War battlefield, the land was that site of the Cotton States and International Exhibition of 1895, which heralded Atlanta and the "new South" to the rest of the country, and was where Booker T. Washington delivered his famous "Cast down your buckets where you are" speech. The site was purchased by the city in 1904.

Over time, five different master plans, including one by the Olmsted Brothers firm in 1912, were prepared and initiated for the park, but none have been completely realized. Despite the overlapping of different schemes, the 189-acre park has remained an English Romantic design of meadows, rolling hills, a lake, and woodlands made up primarily of hardwood trees. Piedmont Park is set within the urban, primarily middle-class, midtown residential area.

Over two million people use the park every year, which attracts a mix of users from the immediate neighborhood, the city at large, and the metropolitan area. As a result, Piedmont Park is a true regional amenity in the center of Atlanta, one particularly valued as the city begins to understand the effects of urban sprawl on its livability. The Atlanta Symphony performs in Piedmont Park in the summer, and several important festivals, including the Peachtree Road Race, Gay Pride, and the Dogwood Festival are held there annually. The park is also home to the Atlanta Botanical Garden.

solicit comments and suggestions to build public support for the planning process and the final master plan, which recommended $25 million in capital improvements to Piedmont Park.

The conservancy followed this work with a three-year strategic plan that identified five major issues as priorities for the park and conservancy (funding, image, programming, membership/stewardship, and operations) and 46 different constituencies. Since then, the Piedmont Park Conservancy has also expressed interest in increasing their involvement in all aspects of park management and has begun to expand its volunteer Ambassador's Program, to provide tree care, weeding, fertilizing, and other maintenance functions.

One lesson the conservancy has learned is the need for continued community input, involvement, and communication. Although the community was heavily involved in the development of the master plan, residents were not involved in the

design for improving Oak Hill, an area of the park's natural landscape identified in the master plan as being in need of environmental conservation and improved accessibility. The design included construction of a viewing area at the park's highest point and secondary paths to improve accessibility for disabled park visitors, among other improvements. When the community reviewed the plans, it objected strongly to the proposed width and design of the paths as well as the viewing area. Believing that the conservancy focused too heavily on "bricks and mortar" and not enough on the strict preservation of turf and trees, a new "Friends of Piedmont Park" was created to fight the plan. A compromise plan, with smaller paths that take a less direct route up the hill was negotiated. "You can't assume anything," says Deb McCown, executive director of the conservancy. "Piedmont Park is a regional park, but the neighborhoods are the ones that are the most impacted." she continued.

McCown describes this experience as part of the learning process, and says she now sees the role of the conservancy as more of a consensus builder—working to make the park a place that is accessible and used by a wide variety of groups. The conservancy now has formed a community committee, which includes the new friends group among other area representatives, and holds meetings on a monthly basis. In addition, McCown reaches out to community groups to keep them informed and involved in what is going on in the park. Before developing the list of priorities for its capital campaign, for example, the conservancy solicited input from the community.

The conservancy's major programs include Junior Park Rangers, an environmental educational program for Pre-K to 12th grade students; Clean and Green, a volunteer program for cleaning and planting in the park; Hands On Atlanta Day in the Park, a volunteer beautifying effort which serves as the major project for Atlanta's recognized community day of service; Park Guides, volunteers who provide walking tours of the park; and Sunday in the Park with the Arts, a free performing arts series with performances by local theater, music, and dance groups.

Name of Park: Piedmont Park

Location: Atlanta, GA

Size: 190 acres

Primary Caretaker: Atlanta Department of Parks, Recreation and Cultural Affairs

---

Name of Organization: Piedmont Park Conservancy

Type: Co-manager

Year Founded: 1989

Staff: 11

Board: 35 members
Ex-Officio and appointed members: Mayor, President of City Council, Parks Commissioner, & 5 Mayoral appointees.

Mission: "To facilitate and contribute to the renewal and preservation of Piedmont Park as a vital, healthy green space and as a cultural and recreational resource which enhances the quality of life for all Atlantans."

Master Plan: 1995

Written Agreements: MOU with the city, 1992

Contact
Deb McCown
Executive Director
Piedmont Park Conservancy
P.O. Box 7795
Atlanta, GA 30357-0795
Phone (404)875-7275
Email: dmccown@mindspring.com

www.piedmontpark.org

───────[**Co-Managers**]───────

Prospect Park Alliance

Brooklyn, New York

Although it is one of Olmsted and Vaux's premier creations, in 1980, Prospect Park was underused and under-performing. That year, there were only 1.7 million visits to the park, and, as park administrator Tupper Thomas points out, that's not many visitors when you consider Brooklyn's size (2.2 million people), lack of public parkland, and the fact that few residents of the borough have a backyard of their own.

In 1980, just after creating the Central Park Administrator's office, Parks Commissioner Gordon Davis created a similar post for Prospect Park. However, in Brooklyn, unlike Manhattan, he included a budget-committing Community Development Block Grant funds to the Prospect Park Administrator's office. The city hired Tupper Thomas, a planner and former official at the New York City Housing and Preservation Department, to be the first park administrator. According to Thomas, she was given four main responsibilities: coordinate the maintenance, recreation, and other functions within the city parks and recreation

department-allowing the department to approach management of the park collectively; initiate a capital program to restore the park and upgrade its neglected facilities; find ways to attract more people to the park; and raise private dollars to augment city dollars.

It soon became clear that in order to raise private dollars, a nonprofit organization would need to be created to take those dollars in, because the private sector was not likely to give money directly to the city. Thomas began an effort to find bankers, businesspeople, stockbrokers, and other influential members of the community to launch the effort. "We wanted folks who could raise private dollars and make people comfortable that their money wasn't going into the black hole of government," she noted. "And we wanted to be taken seriously, as a major cultural entity in the city, like a museum or a botanic garden,"

In 1987, the Prospect Park Alliance was formed as a nonprofit organization in partnership with the parks department and the borough of Brooklyn. The alliance raises private funds for

Baseball game on the Long Meadow, Prospect Park.

Prospect Park | Brooklyn, New York

FREDERICK LAW OLMSTED called it "a sense of enlarged freedom"[19] and it's what you are supposed to feel when you come upon the Long Meadow in Prospect Park. Known as Brooklyn's backyard, the 90-acre meadow—nearly a mile in length—is a gathering place for the entire borough, which comes together collectively and as individuals, to walk their dogs, play soccer or volleyball, fly kites, and engage in countless small interactions and participate in large events.

But the Long Meadow is only a piece of 526-acre Prospect Park, built in the 1870's by Frederick Law Olmsted and Calvert Vaux, several years after the famous duo completed Central Park. Though less well known than its Manhattan neighbor, Prospect Park has a purer, simpler design, with far fewer buildings and roads interfering with the strict enjoyment of nature and the absence of city asphalt, concrete, and noise. In Prospect Park, Olmsted and Vaux gave Brooklyn the three park elements they believed were necessary in large doses-grass, woods, and water. They kept the city and the carriages out by designing a drive that rings the park, but no direct transverses crossing the park.

Prospect Park was designed specifically so that one is enveloped in a natural environment upon entering - trees were planted, and park edges were built up so that the city was completely obscured. Though a few taller apartment buildings are now visible from the park, the effect of escape is still strong. The park's essential function, defined by Olmsted 130 years ago, is its ability to bring people together, in ways and for activities they don't engage in otherwise. "In a park," wrote Olmsted, "the largest provision is required for the human presence. Men must come together, and must be seen coming together.[20]" In the wildly diverse mixture of people and activities that the park attracts, one can assert that Prospect Park works as planned.

The simplicity of the park's elements has allowed residents to contribute to the park's ongoing legacy as the heart of Brooklyn in their own, contemporary ways. In-line skates and titanium bikes have replaced carriages and horses on the park's drives, and a drummer's circle, tai chi, yoga, barbecue, and volleyball are everyday activities. Today the park also contains a bandshell, boathouse, carousel, zoo, and skating rink, several historic structures, and five playgrounds. Leffert's Homestead, an eighteenth century Dutch home, is a children's historic house, with interpretive exhibits, storytelling, and other programs.

Prospect Park is the flagship park of Brooklyn, a borough of New York City with a population of 2.2 million. The park is bordered by a mixture of affluent, middle-income and low-income neighborhoods that include substantial Caribbean, Orthodox Jewish, south Asian, Eastern European, African-American, and Latino populations. The park's latest user survey indicates that its visitors are 45% black, 30% white, 20% Latino, and 5% Asian, and that most come from Brooklyn's lowest-income neighborhoods. The Brooklyn Botanic Garden is a neighbor, as is the Brooklyn Public Library, which sits at the main entrance to the park, on Flatbush Avenue.

....

[19] "Preliminary Report to the Commissioners for Laying Out a Park in Brooklyn, New York: Being a Consideration of Circumstances of Site and Other Conditions Affecting the Design of Public Pleasure Grounds." Schuyler, David and Jane Turner Censer, eds. The Papers of Frederick Law Olmsted, Vol. IV, Johns Hopkins University Press, Baltimore, MD. 1992.

[20]. Ibid.

landscape restoration, capital projects and community programming, as well as overseeing the park's volunteer program. Thomas serves as both the president of the Prospect Park Alliance and as the administrator of the park for the city.

The alliance, in its partnership with the city and with many local organizations, has made substantial progress in restoring and revitalizing Prospect Park. In the first twelve years of its existence, it has helped restore the park's carousel, repaired several of its historic buildings, and rebuilt, and in some cases completely redesigned, its five major playgrounds. In addition, the alliance has raised an endowment of over $2.5 million for the park.

But the organization's real capital energy over the last five years has gone into the park's woodlands, a vital but neglected part of the park. The woodlands, which Thomas likes to call "Brooklyn's last forest," was essential to the Olmsted and Vaux plan, and the area was selected to remain forested because of its large standing population of healthy hardwood trees. A main feature of the original design for the woodlands was the Ravine, which included a meandering brook that babbled by the means of a steam-driven pump. Because of this, and the particulars of the landscape, the 150 acres of woodlands require special care: many trees were dead or nearly so, the forest undergrowth was in poor condition, and erosion and inappropriate use (think mountain bikes) had seriously damaged much of the soil and natural effect of the area. The alliance is now at the end of a five-year, $10 million campaign to completely restore the woodlands to Olmsted's and Vaux's high standards: using archival photographs, it has reconstructed the Ravine, and a large group of volunteers turns out every week to help replant the area with native plants.

The woodlands isn't the only project that receives the support of the park's volunteers. Volunteers have been used in every conceivable capacity since 1991, when the city initiated a 30% budget cut on park maintenance and operations. By 1992, volunteer hours in Prospect Park were up 25%. In one of its more innovative programs, the alliance established a corps of "greeters" in 1996, who stand at the park's entrances and try to guide people to the appropriate area for their activity, such as barbecuing or soccer, while handing out garbage bags and advice, as needed. "Since these are local neighborhood folks who live near that entrance, they recognize people, and they hear and see what is going on. Their feedback has been invaluable," says Thomas. This outreach strategy also encompasses the woodlands, where volunteer guides give regular tours of the work in progress, both to keep interested parkgoers up to date and to help explain to them why such a large area of the park is fenced off, as well as how better stewardship can prevent the damage from happening again.

Weekly, a very reliable cadre of trained volunteers also maintains the park's formal flowerbeds, and lends a hand when needed elsewhere. And an army of Girl Scouts has adopted the park's Concert Grove. Once a month from April through November, they descend on the grove in the hundreds to weed, clean, mulch, rake leaves, and edge pathways. Some of the girls have been working in the grove for years.

The alliance has mastered the art of dealing with large groups, a task not easily accomplished by many nonprofit parks organizations. A large investment bank regularly sends groups to the park to fulfill a community service requirement, and to conduct team-building exercises. These can be small groups of 15-20, which are good for taking on planting projects, or large groups of over 100, who may be sent out to remove invasive plants over a large area. Perhaps the largest single event of all is "You gotta have Park!," a spring fundraising and cleanup event that requires from 750-1,000 volunteers to plan and execute. Volunteers set up at the park's 19 entrances to collect donations, while others participate in a massive cleanup. The event raised over $15,000 for the park in 1999. Other volunteer-organized events, such as the Green-a-Thon, a 6-kilometer walk/run through the park's paths, and the Halloween Festival, attract hundreds of volunteers for the park and participants for its programs.

In outreach and advocacy, the alliance also has a knack with community groups and organizations, finding innovative ways to bring groups together around issues that impact them and the park collectively. For example, the park's neighbors include the Brooklyn Public Library, Brooklyn Museum of Art, and Brooklyn Botanic Garden. Along with the Prospect Park Zoo, a separately-

Tours of the Prospect Park Woodlands educate park users about the alliance's extensive restoration efforts.

managed facility located inside the park's borders, the group has formed a partnership, called "A Day in Brooklyn," that markets these institutions collectively, in part by co-sponsoring a free trolley that runs from one to the other on weekends. Another group with whom the alliance has worked well are the dog owners. When off-leash dogs began to cause a problem in the park, Thomas called the dog owners together, gave them off-leash privileges, and then told them that they had to police themselves in order to keep those privileges. The result, Fellowship for the Interests of Dogs and their Owners, known as FIDO, is recognized as a model for the entire city.

The Community Committee, which represents over 60 organizations—from Haitians to Hasidic Jews—is the park's public voice and the alliance's chief tool for understanding the interests of the diverse neighborhoods that surround Prospect Park. More than just an outreach tool, the community committee is the advocacy arm of the organization. "A strong Community Committee suggests to the politicians that a lot of people aren't going to vote for them if they don't recognize that parks come in either second or third after police and education in terms of the amenities that people think of highly," said Henry Christensen, the alliance's board chairman.[21] Community Committee representatives, including members

of the committee's youth council, make regular visits to Albany and to city council meetings to advocate for the park.

But this, Christensen indicated, goes further, underscoring another role of both the Community Committee, and the alliance, "By having the Community Committee broaden our base as much as possible, it makes sure that the city council is paying a lot more attention to parks in general because the alliance can speak for a lot of parks in Brooklyn, not just for Prospect Park.[22]" (For more on the Prospect Park Community Committee, see Chapter 3). Advocacy has become a more and more important role of the committee, and the alliance, as the city budget for parks has decreased by over 60% since the mid-eighties, when the organization was founded.

The alliance also has control over most of the park concessions. It rents out the park's picnic house and carousel during non-public hours, and runs the pedal-boat and skate rentals at the rink and on the lake, as well as food sales and the gift shop. A private concessionaire runs the skating

[21] "Permanent Partners in Prospect Park," *Parks as Community Places*, Conference Proceedings, San Francisco, CA, 1998. Project for Public Spaces p. 31.

[22] Ibid. p. 31.

school. The alliance gets additional income from movie and commercial shoots. Earned income accounted for over $100,000 in 2000.

The key for Thomas and the alliance is keeping things in the right categories: the parks department, which she represents as the city park administrator, determines park policy. Fundraising and advocacy are the alliance's territory. "Many donors will write to the alliance about problems they see in the park, and I write back on parks department stationary explaining that the board of the alliance and their membership has helped with augment dollars but that the alliance is not involved in any issues—such as closing the loop road to cars, which was a big issue," says Thomas. "The board has always been very clear that they cannot take a stand on issues, because if they start, then the alliance won't be an equal partner with the parks department, which makes policy, operations and rules." Partnership, to the alliance, also means that the nonprofit is raising funds that are incremental to the city's contribution, and that the parks department will remain responsible for basic city services.

Name of Park: Prospect Park

Size: 526 acres

Location: Brooklyn, NY

Primary Caretaker: NYC Department of Parks and Recreation

Name of Organization: Prospect Park Alliance

Type: Co-manager

Year Founded: 1987

Staff: 42

Board: 32 members. Includes 3 Ex-Officio members: the Brooklyn Borough President, a City Council Member, and the Commissioner of Parks and Recreation.

Mission: "The Prospect Park Alliance is a public/private partnership with the city of New York which, through fundraising and advocacy, furthers the restoration and preservation of Prospect Park and the development of the park as a resource for the people of New York City."

Master Plan: None

Partnership Agreements: contract with city to run carousel.

Contact
Prospect Park Alliance
Litchfield Villa
95 Prospect Park West
Brooklyn, NY 11215
Tel: (718)965-8951
info@prospectpark.org

www.prospectpark.org

Maymont Foundation

Richmond, Virginia

The movement to fully restore and manage the Maymont estate began in the 1950's with the Thalhimer-Virginia Wildlife Foundation, an organization that was formed to raise money to build an animal habitat and promote environmental education there. Although the Victorian estate on the James River in Richmond had been bequeathed to the city in 1925, the original owners left no endowment for the continued upkeep and management of the facility. Since maintenance of Maymont's extensively landscaped grounds and formally-decorated home were beyond the means of the city at that time, other needs of the estate, in preservation and conservation, began to come to light as a result of the foundation's efforts.

By 1972, public concern about the deteriorated condition of the park had risen to a point where the foundation and a group of concerned citizens decided that some action needed to be taken. The group approached the city with a proposal to enter into an agreement that would turn over the operations and maintenance of Maymont to the foundation, if it could raise $1 million toward park improvements.

An agreement between the Maymont Foundation and the city, however, was not reached easily. While the city council was in favor of this proposal, the Richmond Department of Parks and Recreation was more hesitant: it considered Maymont the gem of the city's parks system. The city council was also concerned that an agreement of this type might violate the stipulation in the Dooley's will that the park remain under city ownership or else revert to the Dooley's heirs. The foundation hired a lawyer to construct an agreement that would allow its involvement to be legal, and during the course of developing this agreement, revised and expanded the charter of the Thalhimer-Virginia Foundation and renamed the organization The Maymont Foundation. In 1972, the city adopted an ordinance stipulating that upon approval of

the contract by the court, the foundation would be required to raise $1 million dollars by June 1973. If this were done, the city would enter into an operating agreement with the foundation.

Continued resistance from the department of parks and recreation held up the matter in court, and the Maymont Foundation, concerned that its time was running out to raise the required $1 million, brought a lawsuit against the city to have the agreement approved. The court approved the agreement later that year, and the city council extended the foundation's time to raise the money until December 1974.

The foundation then set about organizing a campaign to raise the necessary $1 million with the leadership of a local real estate developer, a member of the city planning commission, and the wife of the elder Thalhimer son serving as the campaign's chair. With the money successfully raised, a 30-year operating agreement between the city and the Maymont Foundation was signed in 1975 that turned over management of the park to the foundation. The agreement also specified that the city would provide the foundation with an annual subsidy of $125,000, the amount the city was currently allocating for the upkeep of the estate. The foundation was required to spend the $1 million it had raised over the following three years in accordance with a 1971 master plan it had developed. The agreement also ensured that the foundation would keep the park open and free to the public, and that the city would help with tree work and other basic city services. That same year, a master plan was developed for the rehabilitation of Maymont that included improvements to the animal habitat and restoration of the historic buildings and gardens.

The Maymont Foundation operates and maintains the park with almost astonishing independence. Having privately managed the park for over 25 years, the Maymont Foundation is viewed as being extremely competent in its duties as caretakers of the property. There is no day-to-day working

Maymont | Richmond, Virginia

MAYMONT, A 100-acre Victorian-era estate, was originally the home of Major and Mrs. James Henry Dooley, one of Richmond's most prominent families. The Dooleys had extensively landscaped the grounds and built a large Victorian house filled with an impressive collection of furnishings and decorative arts when the entire estate was left intact to the city of Richmond upon the death of Mrs. Dooley in 1925. Maymont was opened to the public as a park and museum in 1925, and quickly became a major civic attraction, hosting events such as a Christmas celebration when the house and grounds are decorated as they would have been in 1893, replete with carolers and carriage rides.

The original park included formal gardens, an arboretum, the Dooley's home, and a carriage house, stone barn, and other outbuildings. In 1942, William B. Thalhimer, the CEO of a family-owned department store, created an exhibit of Virginia wildlife habitats, a mini-zoo of sorts, at Maymont. In 1959, more permanent and improved wildlife and outdoor habitat exhibits were funded by the Thalhimer-Virginia Wildlife Foundation, and in 1962, a local horticultural society converted a stone barn on the property into a nature center. In 1982, a children's farm was built exhibiting domestic animals. A new 26,000 square foot nature and visitor's center opened to the public in November, 1999.

Maymont is bounded on two sides by additional city parkland. A third side of the estate abuts the James River. Two residential neighborhoods are near Maymont. The east side is a middle class and predominately African-American neighborhood, and the north side is predominantly white and upper-middle class. Approximately 400,000 visitors come to the park each year, 70% of them from the immediate region.

relationship with the city, although there is periodic consultation usually around the topic of capital projects. Park policies are developed by the foundation, and as long as the park remains "free and open to the public," the parks and recreation department stays uninvolved in management. However, the director of the parks and recreation department, a city council member, and a representative of the city planning commission sit on the foundation's board, and all major capital improvements in the park require approval by the city planning commission.

Certainly, a key reason for this independence is the foundation's ability to raise money and maintain the estate to the highest standard. For example, the foundation recently completed a $17.5 million capital campaign to build a combined visitor's and nature center that included $4.5 million earmarked for the new building's endowment. The foundation has an annual operat-

ing budget of approximately $2.5 million, most of which is raised through earned income. One source of this is the Maymont Flower and Garden Show, which is organized and hosted by the foundation, attracts in excess of 30,000 visitors, and raises $200,000. Held in the city's downtown convention center, the show makes a major economic contribution to the city as a whole.

The Maymont Foundation's relationship with the parks and recreation department remained rocky until the early 1980's, when new personnel assumed the leading positions at the department as well as at the city management level. However, the amount of the city's annual appropriation to the Maymont Foundation has remained an issue—even though the contribution has risen to between $200-$300,000—since the park's basic operational expenses have continued to rise.

In 1995, the foundation's original operating agreement with the city was renewed with some

JAY PAUL

Italian Garden, Maymont.

minor revisions. After almost five years, the foundation is once again embarking on renegotiating parts of their contract with the city. Geoffrey Platt, Jr., the Maymont Foundation's executive director, would like to move toward a formulaic way of figuring out the city's annual contribution, so that the foundation doesn't have to struggle every year with the city council about the amount of city funds it receives. He would like the city to recognize its partnership with the foundation through increased financial support.

The other operational funds to run the park come primarily from fundraising activities and other government subsidies. Since Maymont also serves as a regional asset, two adjacent counties and the state of Virginia make annual voluntary contributions toward the foundation's operational expenses. The foundation is also building an endowment for the park, which, at the time of this writing, was valued at $300,000.

Name of Park: Maymont

Size: 100 acres

Location: Richmond, Virginia

Primary Caretaker: The Maymont Foundation

Name of Organization: Maymont Foundation

Type: Sole manager

Year Founded: 1975

Staff: 56 staff persons (full and part-time)

Board: 49 members. Includes 3 Ex-Officio members: from the City Council, Planning Commission and Director of Recreation and Parks, 5 appointed from other organizations.

Mission: "The mission of the Maymont Foundation is to provide in Maymont Park, traditionally an area of beauty in an urban setting, educational, recreational and cultural opportunities for the people of metropolitan Richmond through the restoration and development of Maymont, including its museums, animal exhibits, gardens and other resources."

Master Plan: 1975, and 1995

Partnership Agreements: MOU with the city of Richmond.

Contact
Kate Peeples
Director of Public Affairs
1700 Hampton Street
Richmond, VA 23220
804/358-7166
kpeeples@maymont.org

www.maymont.org

Yakima Greenway Foundation

Yakima, Washington

The Yakima Greenway Foundation, like many non-profit parks organizations, was the product of years of failed attempts at preserving the Yakima River Corridor. Frank Frederick, a Yakima resident who wrote a 150-page narrative history of the greenway, counted nine separate attempts to create a green-way from Union Gap to Selah Gap beginning in the 1940's. But though each effort to convince the city, county, or state to protect the corridor was a failure individually, the sum of the total was suc-cess. Over time, greenway advocates moved into positions of power, and opponents stepped down. Eventually, enough critical mass was gathered for the city of Yakima to commission a master plan that was adopted in 1976, though neither the city nor Yakima County had funds to bring the project to fruition.

But the plan was a vision, and a vision can inspire. Advocates and conservationists in the region developed slide shows and gave talks to important political and environmental figures. Finally, the project was launched with a whimper rather than a bang in 1979, when the Yakima city council passed the ball to the county, and the county recommended the formation of a task force to explore organizing a foundation to imple-ment and maintain a greenway, and implement the master plan. With the major private sector leaders in the room, a greenway task force became a board of directors, and the Yakima Greenway Foundation was established in 1980. Acting on the advice of a regional representative from the Trust for Public Land, the board used the model of a land trust, and began to acquire property along the river.

Because of its origins as a land trust, preserva-tion of the corridor was the first real mission of the foundation, but without a recreational agenda, the movement lacked the needed interest from residents. In a less-densely populated area like the Yakima Valley, where open space is not at a premi-um, people have to see the value of a new area in terms of how they might be able to use it, as well as its value as a preserve. So the new foundation began to push on the recreational possibilities of the corridor and started building the greenway earlier than it originally had planned. This proved to be a winning formula and presaged a general shift from preservation to recreation among the foundation's board.

A private, nonprofit organization, the founda-tion is responsible for developing, maintaining and operating greenway facilities and encouraging conservation throughout the greenway corridor. While the city and county wholeheartedly support the greenway as a regional amenity, neither has any real administrative oversight of the area. Although some of the greenway is on city and county land, the land is loaned to the foundation. Explicit in the foundation's formation was the con-cept that the greenway would present no financial burden on the city or county. "They [the city and county] couldn't maintain it or pay for it then, and they still won't," said Cecilia Vogt, former execu-tive director of the Yakima Greenway Foundation. However Vogt added that both municipalities cooperate fully with the foundation, and do pro-vide considerable support, including actively seek-ing state grants for the greenway and partnering with the foundation to get them.

Since the city and county of Yakima have offi-cially adopted the master plan, they recognize that all work in the corridor must conform to the plan and consult with the foundation regularly on proj-ects that they believe may impact the greenway. Since the Yakima Greenway is not part of the county or city parks systems, the foundation has sole responsibility for the greenway and for setting greenway policy, raising all monies needed to man-age, program, and maintain the area, through rev-enues from its own bingo hall, fundraising events, donations from local service clubs, memorials, reservation fees for certain greenway facilities, and

Yakima Greenway | Yakima, Washington

The Yakima Greenway runs along the Yakima and Naches Rivers and is bordered by the Union Gap to the south and the Selah Gap to the north. The Yakima Greenway is not part of the city or county park system, although several connector trails from it to other parks within those systems are being built or have been completed.

The current 10-mile asphalt greenway is made up of three large recreational areas, three conservation areas, and one natural area with a combined total of roughly 400 acres, though only 100 are actively maintained and used. The greenway's center of gravity is Sarg Hubbard Park, which contains a visitors center, a stage, a physical fitness course, war memorials, maintenance and picnic facilities, restrooms, and access to the Yakima River. Many other locations combine parks, picnic areas, places for fishing, playgrounds, and river access.

Sitting in the reflection of Mount Rainier, the Yakima valley's microclimate makes for extraordinarily good weather. The valley has an annual average of 300 days of sunshine and just 8.00 inches of precipitation, nearly half of which is snow. Extensive irrigation has transformed the valley from a desert into an agricultural center. According to 1997 US Census estimates, approximately 218,000 people live within Yakima County. The area surrounding the greenway is characterized by large percentages of low-income residents and migrant workers.

memberships. An endowment campaign is currently underway with $1.2 million raised to date and $10 million targeted by 2005.

Because of the well-publicized role the greenway plays in the lives of Yakima residents, and the ever-growing network of trails and connections to and from other parks and trails, many residents do not even know that the greenway receives no city or county funding. "They think it's part of the parks system," says Vogt, who notes that this misconception can be a hindrance to fundraising. "It is important that they understand that the foundation raises all the funds, so I made that a key part of our message."

The strategy to permanently endow park operations, instead of annually raising funds, was adopted several years ago because of a major crisis afflicting the foundation's bottom line: the collapse of revenues from a state licensed bingo hall, operated at a sight off the greenway, that had accounted for over half of their annual income annually. The bingo hall was the foundation's cash cow for five years, but competition from gambling

operations on a local Indian Reservation has caused revenues to drop by over 75%. Needless to say, the loss of the bingo funds was a major blow to the foundation, which now operates with a budget shortfall while it tries to find alternative sources of income, make its events more profitable, and raise the endowment.

Endowment funds are being solicited from individuals and corporations, "the same twenty major donors the foundation relies upon to raise the annual budget," said Vogt, who told these donors that she wouldn't have to return and ask the following year if they were willing to give more to fund the endowment. "Our goal," she adds, "is to raise $10 million, but if the foundation had $3 million, we could replace the revenues from the bingo hall completely."

Income-producing festivals also greatly define the greenway for residents, and are a key source of revenue. The way the foundation runs them demonstrates nicely the marketing leverage parks can provide for vendors. During the "A Case of the Blues" festival, a popular live music event, not only

The 10-mile Yakima Greenway is managed and maintained entirely by the Yakima Greenway Foundation.

is there an admission fee, but local beer breweries and wine makers pay the foundation to let their employees come and pour drinks for the public. In addition, the manufacturers sell the beer at cost to the foundation, which can then make a profit on each drink poured. The Great Yakima Duck Race, another popular event, is a raffle that generates in excess of $20,000 for the foundation, and $20,000 for their partners, each year. Local businesses and citizens buy tickets in the form of small, numbered, rubber ducks, which are placed in the Yakima River at a point along the greenway with thousands of others. The first duck to float to the finish line is the winner, and the holder of that

duck's number in the raffle is awarded a sizable prize (one year it was a pickup truck). In addition to these events, the foundation also hosts an Earth Day celebration, which is run in conjunction with their environmental education program.

Four full-time maintenance workers open the greenway gates, clean restrooms, empty trash receptacles, fertilize, water, and mow the lawns, erase graffiti, and pick up litter. However, many of these tasks, as long as they do not involve heavy equipment, are also done by volunteers and by seniors (see "Remedial Maintenance" section).

The greenway continues to grow, although not necessarily in length. Recently, a consortium of youth leagues that needed a new baseball facility and hoped to build it on foundation land approached the foundation. The leagues have received a grant to begin construction, and the foundation will compel them to pay for maintenance of the facility once it is built, so that the ballpark will be entirely self-maintaining. In addition, connector trails to city and county parks and greenways are in various stages of planning and construction, and one link may eventually connect the greenway with Puget Sound, approximately 150 miles away.

Name of Park: Yakima Greenway

Location: Yakima, Washington

Size: 400 acres, 10 miles of paved trails

Primary Caretaker: Yakima Greenway Foundation

Name of Organization: Yakima Greenway Foundation

Year Formed: 1980

Type: Sole manager

Staff: 8

Board: Maximum of 25 members

Mission: "The purpose of the Yakima Greenway Foundation is to conserve, enhance and maintain the Yakima Greenway as a continuing living resource for future generations."

Master Plan: 1976, by Jones and Jones. First update, 1985, second 1991, third, 1995

Written Agreements: Management/ maintenance agreements with city of Yakima and Yakima County

Contact
Al Brown
Yakima Greenway Foundation
111 South 18th Street
Yakima, Washington 98901
Tel: (509)453-8280
greenway@nwinfo.net

co.yakima.wa.us/greenway/gwmain.htm

Partnerships for Parks

New York City, New York
Deep in the throes of a 20-year fiscal crisis, with the budget for parks and recreation slashed by over 60% since 1980, only parks with strong community representation have been able to garner the attention and maintenance necessary to keep them vital and healthy in New York City. Understanding the relationship between a strong local constituency and public funding and attention, Parks Commissioner Henry J. Stern and the City Parks Foundation formed Partnerships for Parks in 1995, as a joint venture between the two organizations.

"The idea behind Partnerships for Parks," says Tim Tompkins, Partnerships' director and founder, "is to mobilize neighborhood residents to advocate for, and take stewardship of, their local parks." Because most of the city's smaller parks cannot raise the private dollars and afford the extra maintenance staff that the Central Park Conservancy can. Partnerships, as the group is known citywide, spends most of its funds on staff who encourage the formation, and nurture the development of, parks advocacy groups across the city, and organize volunteers to participate in citywide clean up and greening events. To further local support networks, Partnerships also awards small grants to neighborhood organizations.

But while other citywide advocacy groups could fit this description, the way Partnerships for Parks is organized is unique. For one thing, it is not an organization: it is a partnership between a nonprofit and the city. The staff shares offices with the Department of Parks and Recreation, and Partnerships' $2 million operating budget is funded jointly by the city and from private and corpo-

Marcus Garvey Park on Big Help Day, a city wide event, sponsored by Nickelodeon and coordinated by Partnerships for Parks.

BENJAMIN SWETT

rate donations. The City Parks Foundation, a non-profit, 501(c)(3) organization that raises private funds for parks and playgrounds in the city, handles the private donations and foundation support that provide the salaries and benefits for 40% of Partnerships for Parks' 32 staff members including the director. The other 60% of the staff are city employees, although they report to Tompkins.

Therefore, while most advocacy groups operate at arm's length from the public sector, in the case of Partnerships for Parks the opposite is true. If it seems odd that a parks commissioner would provide room and salaries for 15 staff members of an advocacy organization, then one can think of the partnership as the volunteer arm of the city parks department. However, this group does much more than organize volunteers.

Partnerships' staff nurtures local park groups through direct outreach and assistance. Outreach coordinators in the boroughs provide a link to the parks department for community and friends groups, and offer workshops and training materials, everything from "How to Start a Friends Group" to "Tips on Planning Special Events." In only five years, the organization's outreach coordinators and staff have attended over 6,000 community meetings, and provided more than 120 workshops. In 1999, the organization held 140 separate events.

Partnerships for Parks also has launched five "catalyst" park projects in neighborhoods that have particularly viable parks; but no organized leadership. In these parks, catalyst coordinators conduct programs and events and attempt to build a constituency. They also have conducted rigorous surveys and analyses in an attempt to create models

New York City Parks System | New York City, New York

Although New York is the largest city in the United States, its park system is smaller, both in acreage and in budget, than that of many other American cities. Not that it is a small system: the New York City Department of Parks and Recreation oversees 28,000 acres of open and recreational spaces, consisting of more than 1,500 parks, playgrounds, and recreation facilities across the five boroughs of Manhattan, The Bronx, Brooklyn, Queens, and Staten Island, including beaches, swimming pools, golf courses, and ice rinks, and nearly 2 million park trees. The Department of Parks and Recreation had a combined capital and expense budget of approximately $400 million in 1999.

However, the staff of the parks department is one-third what it was in 1970, and the department's operating budget continues to be cut. With no infusion of public funds in the offing, the Department of Parks and Recreation has had to find new sources of funds itself, and ways of doing more with less.

New York City has every conceivable kind of park—from small triangles in busy intersections to tidal salt marshes, ocean beaches, neighborhood gardens converted from vacant lots, formal squares, and major urban parks. There is an equal number of ways these parks are managed with varying degrees of public and private support, partnerships with community groups, and strategies for generating stewardship, vitality, and income. The Department of Parks and Recreation estimates that tens of thousands of people are active in over 250 "Friends of the Park" groups, as well as over 1,000 other civic groups that contribute to their parks in some way throughout the year, including the Central Park Conservancy, the Prospect Park Alliance, and the Riverside Park Fund.

Under the leadership of Commissioner Henry J. Stern, several innovations have been instituted, including the use of nearly 6,000 welfare recipients as park maintenance workers at no cost to the department (their salaries are paid by public assistance); a dramatic inspection program, which began in the city's playgrounds and is now being instituted throughout the system; and an effort to "green" traffic islands and other slivers of public space by planting trees or shrubs and eliciting the help of neighbors to care for these new spaces, known as the Greenstreets program. Over 800 traffic islands and medians to date have flowered under this program.

The parks department also has aggressively acquired land, nearly 2,000 acres of it since 1994, when Commissioner Stern took the helm. Much of this land was industrial, located along rivers and other waterfronts. Some of it was handed over to the parks department by other city agencies, primarily the Department of Transportation.

for revitalizing neighborhood parks across the city, and to test and document different methodologies.

Two other catalyst projects that Partnerships has launched take on the specific issue of restoring and revitalizing waterfronts. The Astoria Waterfront Arts program tries to attract the diverse communities located near the Queens waterfront—an area with immense environmental, logistical, and other challenges—to arts programs, such as outdoor films, in the string of waterfront parks separating Queens from Manhattan. The Waterways & Trailways program, a collaboration with the

BENJAMIN SWETT

A catch and release fishing program in Crotona Park, the Bronx.

National Park Service and the Appalachian Mountain Club, organizes events and is restoring the natural areas, such as the Bronx River, in the hundreds of potential waterfront access points in the New York City's neighborhoods.

Partnerships organizes two major citywide volunteer events: "It's My Park!," a green-up day, held in late May, and Clean-up Day, held in October. For these events, the staff coordinates thousands of volunteers who are sent into over 200 different parks across the city. Newspapers, radio stations and television affiliates promote the events through public service announcements and, in addition to other helpful sponsorships, Wendy's Restaurant displays registration boxes at 192 locations. The events also receive in-kind donations of paint, garbage bags, and bins.

"It's My Park!" is more than a volunteer event; it is a full-bore media campaign. In 1997, a national advertising firm helped Partnerships to develop the slogan and a logo. Mugs, t-shirts, key chains, refrigerator magnets, water bottles, and Frisbees are distributed to volunteers and sold via the parks department's ParkStore. "'It's My Park!' is the central message of our media campaign," said Tompkins. "It encourages people to appreciate and take on more responsibility for conditions in their neighborhood parks."

In addition to these citywide events, Partnerships' volunteer coordinators provide linkages between parks in need and other volunteer groups in the city, such as New York Cares. High visibility projects, the most appealing kind to corporations, are marketed as both teambuilding and giving opportunities. Corporations sometimes donate supplies as well as cash, and provide volunteer workers to stabilize eroding slopes, edge sidewalks, repair fences, and re-seed lawns.

But the real volunteers are the residents who watch over the parks and become their true stewards. Recognition of these community leaders is a mainstay for Partnerships, which celebrates the efforts of community groups and volunteers in several ways. It makes the city parks commissioner available at regular breakfasts, luncheons, and other receptions to meet local leaders and hear their suggestions and accomplishments, and holds regular "thank you" events on the roof of the Arsenal, the 19th century building in Central Park that houses the parks department offices.

Partnerships for Parks also recognizes volunteers by issuing the "Parks Card," which serves as a sort of membership card for a park. "The Metropolitan Museum of Art has 102,000 people who are members. And they have a particular identification with that museum," said New York City Parks Commissioner Henry Stern. "We want people to be able to join the parks-a particular park-and feel that by doing that they're a user. That they have a particular linkage to that park, a responsibility for it. It creates a tangible—if small—connection to parks that people carry around in their wallet."[23] As "membership" grows, Partnerships for Parks is able to broker discounts with local businesses and other advantages for cardholders. For example, some museums offer 2-for-1 admissions to cardholders, several restaurants offer a complimentary beverage, and stores offer significant discounts on select days.

Another key factor for Partnerships for Parks is the development of an extensive database, which has become something of an obsession for Tompkins. "Millions of people come to New York City's parks every year, but only recently have we attempted to capture and nurture their interest more effectively, and use this to build a constituency for parks in New York," said Tompkins, whose list is up to 45,000 names. In building the database, Tompkins collects the names of everyone who calls the parks department to report an incident, complain about a broken bench, or ask how

---

[23] "Rating New York's Playgrounds," Parks as Community Places, Conference Proceedings, Boston, MA 1997. (Urban Parks Institute, 1997.) p 26

to get a tennis permit. "Our park rangers had five thousand names of people who had gone on park tours over the past few years, but those lists were just sitting in a file," he explained. Other sources included the permitting office, which had several thousand names and addresses of people who had applied for permits to hold events in city parks, park and neighborhood groups that gave their membership lists, and soccer leagues that regularly played in city parks.

Since Partnerships holds hundreds of events, meetings, and workshops annually, every staff member is instructed to circulate a sign-in sheet at any meeting a staff member attends or hosts. In addition, a raffle is held at many events to encourage people to submit their names and addresses for the database. Tompkins considers the list-which can be sorted by affiliation, borough, type of organization, even interest level and commitment to park issues-to be a key advocacy tool. "The core idea behind this is that for most parks in most neighborhoods, especially poorer ones, public dollars are what is needed to adequately maintain parks, since only a handful of parks can raise significant private money. The way to make that happen is to create local and citywide constituencies for parks. When that constituency is mobilized, resources and opportunities can be seized, whether through a referendum, or a bond issue, or by influencing budget priorities. The database is our attempt to build and coalesce this constituency." Everyone in the database receives a copy of Partnerships for Parks' monthly newsletter, The Leaflet.

Tompkins admits that the organizing principles behind this constituency building exercise are explicitly political, adding that he wants the group to begin to influence local elections by mobilizing his list to support candidates that support a parks-friendly agenda. Because Partnerships is significantly funded with public money, this has to be done in partnership with another advocacy organization that could be more aggressive on behalf of parks and open spaces.

Name of Park: New York City Parks System

Location: New York City

Size: 28,181 acres

Primary Caretaker: New York City Department of Parks and Recreation

---

Name of Organization: Partnerships for Parks

Type: Citywide

Year Formed: 1995

Mission: "At Partnerships for Parks, we believe that parks are essential to the life of the city, and that community involvement is essential to the life of a park. We have seen that the parks that thrive, rather than simply survive, are those that have active communities caring and fighting for them. Our mission is to spur more community support for and involvement in New York City's parks. We work to strengthen, support and start neighborhood park groups; link them together so that they can learn from each other and be stronger collectively; and promote parks in general so that people will be more likely to join in efforts to restore and preserve them."

Staff: 32

Board: There are 30 members of the City Parks Foundation board not including the city parks commissioner, who serves ex-officio.

Master Plan: NA

Written Agreements: None

Contact:
Dana Littvack
Deputy Director for Central Operations
The Arsenal
Central Park
New York, NY 10021
(212) 360-8120
violet@parklan.nycnet.ci.cn.nyc.us

www.partnershipsforparks.org

Philadelphia Green

Philadelphia, Pennsylvania

The Pennsylvania Horticultural Society, founded in 1827, is one of the country's leading organizations in helping city residents improve their quality of life through horticulture. The Society is well known for the annual Philadelphia Flower Show (the world's largest indoor flower show) and other events, such as the yearly City Gardens Contest. With a staff of 110, it also publishes a monthly color magazine and two newsletters and runs a public library of 15,000 items on horticulture. Aside from the sheer scale of these operations, what distinguishes the Society from other horticultural organizations is its devout commitment to helping low-income residents improve their surroundings and actively participate in the revitalization of blighted areas, through its Philadelphia Green program.

The Philadelphia Green program's origins lie in a 1974 experiment, when a pilot community garden program attempted to put Philadelphia's abundant vacant land to better use. Inspired by the level of community participation and feedback, the Society launched the Philadelphia Green program four years later, with a block grant of $250,000 from the city Office of Housing and Community Development, to work with community groups and residents in neighborhoods throughout the city to transform their neighborhoods, providing plants, construction materials, technical assistance, and workshops in garden and tree care. Since then, Philadelphia Green has grown to a staff of 50 and an annual budget of approximately $4 million, and offers a broad range of programs, from fundraising workshops for community groups to school programs that promote stewardship among young people. Working with over 1,100 neighborhood groups, government organizations, and corporations, the program has been involved in nearly 2,500 greening projects in Philadelphia, and lays claim to the title nation's largest community greening program. Today over 50% of

Philadelphia Green's programming is funded by foundations, with another 25% funded by proceeds from the Philadelphia Flower Show (which generates approximately $1.4 million each year for the Society).

In 1993, with twenty years' experience in engaging neighborhoods in the renewal of their streetscapes, Philadelphia Green launched a new project that bridged the needs of park friends groups and the sorely underfunded recreation department. Beginning with a major grant from the William Penn Foundation, Philadelphia Green developed the Parks Revitalization Project, an initiative to revitalize small neighborhood parks into hubs of community activity by providing technical assistance to citizens groups to plan, develop, and maintain their local parks. The project is being undertaken in partnership with the Department of Recreation to introduce better maintenance practices and prioritize small capital projects, based on community input. Philadelphia Green has secured funding from the Penn Foundation and the Wallace-Reader's Digest Fund for the project, with the Department of Recreation providing matching funds for the Wallace Funds grant.

Over the last several years this partnership has made a visible difference in nine pilot parks where the Department of Recreation and Philadelphia Green together have provided community groups with encouragement, organizational assistance, plant materials, and expertise. In 1999, the Parks Revitalization Project expanded to include 24 parks citywide. Maitreyi Roy, a Program Manager for Philadelphia Green, remembers when one of the parks, Norris Square, was a center of illegal activity where cars were dumped, trees set on fire, and gunfire was routine. Beginning in the 1980s, community groups such as the Norris Square Neighborhood Project began to work with federal, state and local agencies to raze dilapidated structures, organize neighborhood volunteers, and recover the park. In 1993, Philadelphia Green

Local youth chips-in on a "workday" in Mario Lanza Park, Queen Village, Philadelphia

became part of a multi-year renovation of the park, providing horticultural staff for tree planting and pruning, removing dead trees, and paying contractors to strip graffiti. "In the beginning, there were just two of us from Philadelphia Green who worked with the Norris Square Neighborhood Project (a youth/environmental community organization)," says Roy. "Working with the group, and other residents, we started some small targeted early action projects that resulted in more people getting involved. Together, we got a lot accomplished by going to the neighborhood kids, who would then get their parents involved."

Philadelphia Green also negotiated an agreement with the Department of Streets to make regular garbage pick-ups at the park, instead of leaving that duty to the overstretched recreation department. With the Norris Square

Neighborhood Project, they organized workshops where residents and youth designed and helped install a new playground, seating areas and a pavilion. The Department of Recreation committed additional funds for the capital improvements and supervised the playground's construction. For the pavilion, ceramic tiles were designed and fired by residents, who organized a night vigil to guard the tiles in case vandals tried to move them before the mortar dried. According to Roy, "along with regular cleanups, we planned a variety of more permanent projects. Community designed art work not only gave Norris Square a unique sense of place but also built a sense of ownership among the teenagers in the neighborhood." Routinely, local volunteers organized by the Norris Square Neighborhood Project clean the park, as do groups from the United Way and Americorps, contacted by way of the connections made through local CDCs and Philadelphia Green.

The credit for the success of this and other projects is due, in large part, to the members Philadelphia Green's field staff, who are on a first name basis with neighborhood residents and are plainly committed to developing personal as well as working relationships. Joint projects with other community organizations also have thrived by virtue of the commitment from field staff. "People respond when someone helps make their efforts seem manageable," according to John Carpenter, former director of the New Kensington CDC. In a highly successful partnership to revitalize the blighted New Kensington community, "Philadelphia Green provided a full-time staff liaison who had knowledge of Philadelphia Green and its programs, cooperated totally with New Kensington CDC, and who knew what would or would not work."

Philadelphia Green recognizes that the Parks Revitalization Project hinges on a three-way partnership with local groups and the Recreation Department. By strengthening friends groups and developing new initiatives with the Department of Recreation, Philadelphia Green and the city feel there is the potential to introduce this partnership approach to park revitalization system-wide. Indeed, the project's recent expansion to 24 parks represents a step in this direction. Further, the project's long-term success depends on finding a formula for creating local organizational capacity and a stable volunteers corps that can maintain the improvements in neighborhood parks.

Philadelphia Green sees its role as helping friends groups learn how to fundraise, plan events, coordinate horticultural improvements, and organize volunteers so that they can eventually become local stewards. Another focus in recent years has been to aid these groups in developing valuable collaborations and partnerships with community-based organizations and institutions-helping to ensure the long-term stability of these park reclamation efforts.

Selecting the nine pilot parks in 1996 depended on an application process that was in some ways agonizing, partly because there were so many parks that applied for the three-year grants, and also because Philadelphia Green was torn between its desire to help the most needy neighborhoods and the acknowledgement that its work is more sustainable in parks that already have a strong friends group in place. Philadelphia Green addressed this conflict by selecting a variety of parks to participate in the project, including Fairhill Park, which had no friends group at all. In fact, it was Philadelphia Green's call for applications that catalyzed a group of neighbors to organize themselves specifically in order to apply to the project. Roy admits it was a risk to work with such a group that had no history, "but we felt we could afford a few risks and that we would learn more about the ingredients of success by working within a variety of circumstances."

Fairhill Park's biggest lesson for the organization was that it had to have the right tools in its toolbox for different communities. "You can only do so many things with a hammer," says Joan Reilly, another Philadelphia Green Program Manager. At Fairhill, the leadership of the community challenged the way Philadelphia Green was accustomed to organizing projects and building consensus-meetings at Fairhill follow a Quaker model-and decision-making is often an involved process. Nevertheless, the transformation has been as great as in any other park: trees have been planted, an abandoned building removed, a derelict play area referred to as "the bunker" was replaced, and a far wider section of the public has begun to use the park.

Philadelphia Green also has learned that a three-year grant cycle may have discouraged the sort of short-term actions that get the ball rolling, and they recently has changed to giving their grants and assistance on an annual basis instead, with more frequent evaluations and progress reports.

So far, the friends groups involved in the Parks Revitalization Project have raised approximately $500,000 in additional support from private foundations and local businesses, and have received commitments for approximately $700,000 of capital improvements from the Philadelphia City Council. That is considerable leverage of the $15,000 average capital expenditure invested by Philadelphia Green for each of the 24 parks in the Project (plus the extensive staff and office support). The groups are also developing relationships with their local hospitals, churches, and

Working closely with a local community organization, Philadelphia Green helped residents beautify and revitalize Norris Square.

other institutions that help support various improvements and activities at the parks.

In 1998, Philadelphia Green created the Parks in Progress Steering Committee, made up of representatives from the friends groups. The committee is a networking mechanism that encourages cross-fertilization of ideas and strategies and is fast becoming a city-wide advocacy group for parks in Philadelphia. In addition to advocacy, the group is also sharing strategies on community involvement, park safety, education, public commitment, events and publicity. In 1999, Philadelphia Green started its Parks Resource Center, which provides workshops for the friends groups on skill-building, leadership development, fundraising, and park maintenance.

The Department of Recreation has been an enthusiastic supporter of Philadelphia Green, as the program and its local partners create maintenance plans, enlist volunteers and support from local institutions, plan for capital improvements with local input, and make capital improvements to park facilities and landscapes. While the department often will imple-

Philadelphia Green sees its role as helping friends groups learn how to fundraise, plan events, coordinate horticultural improvements, and organize volunteers so that they can eventually become local stewards.

ment the physical improvements, such as building a playground or fixing a drainage problem, equally often Philadelphia Green will make the improvements themselves or hire a local contractor from the neighborhood. Clearly, the department has confidence in its nonprofit partner's abilities. More than that, it even has invited Philadelphia Green to provide training to its staff in better horticulture and maintenance practices.

The climate that made such an arrangement appealing has as much to do with the tribulations of Philadelphia parks and the Department of Recreation as with the emergence of a citywide program like Philadelphia Green. Decades of population loss have left Philadelphia riddled with vacant lots that compromise the cohesiveness of its neighborhoods and reduce the city tax base. In 1998 the United States Census estimated that Philadelphia's population had fallen below 1910

levels - a loss of more than 500,000 people, or about 28%, since its high in 1960.

The effect on the Department of Recreation was nearly disastrous: until Philadelphia Green's engagement in parks, the city nearly had written off any major initiatives to improve neighborhood parks, many of which were in such disrepair that only the playground equipment distinguished them from the surrounding vacant land. Capital spending on parks plummeted from more than $31 million in 1995 to $12 million in 1998. At one point, the Department of Recreation was even on the verge of relinquishing responsibility over them to another city agency. But with new leadership, and the acknowledged success of community greening as a contributing factor in combating urban blight, the department has seen a significant increase in its capital budget, and has enjoyed the autonomy and flexibility needed to be more responsive to the city's neighborhoods.

The Department of Recreation is enthusiastic about collaborating with Philadelphia Green even more in the future, seeing it as an opportunity to put the department in closer contact with community residents, help prioritize capital projects, and even coordinate maintenance between the Department and community volunteers. This would build on Philadelphia Green's strengths in community organizing and building friends groups, with a new emphasis from the city on programming that builds community stewardship. "Recreation staff love working on these innovative projects that give them more ties with the community," according to former Recreation Director Mike DiBerardinis, who presided over the department's growth into a partnership with Philadelphia Green. The department has recently created a new position specifically to work within the partnership and help develop more community partnerships and friends groups.

Name: Philadelphia Parks System

Location: Philadelphia, Pennsylvania

Size: N/A

Primary Caretaker: Philadelphia Department of Recreation

Name of Organization: Pennsylvania Horticultural Society, Philadelphia Green's Parks Revitalization Project

Type: Citywide Partner

Year Formed: Philadelphia Green program: 1978; Pennsylvania Horticultural Society founded in 1827.

Mission: The Pennsylvania Horticultural Society is a not-for-profit membership organization that motivates people to improve the quality of life and create a sense of community through horticulture.

Staff: Philadelphia Green program, with 50 staff, is the largest urban greening program in the country. The Pennsylvania Horticulture Society, as a whole, employs 110 people.

Board: The governing body of the Pennsylvania Horticultural Society is the Council, comprising up to 40 people of diverse backgrounds, including representation of law firms, investment advisors, the press, landscaping companies, garden clubs, philanthropic organizations, the City Planning Commission, major arts institutions, consultants, and individuals. The Council has general charge of the affairs, funds, and property of the Society and has full power to carry out the purposes of the Society, through the PHS staff. The Philadelphia Green program also has its own advisory board of approximately 40 constituents of the program, including members of community organizations, friends groups, and activists. It is used to provide input on Philadelphia Green's future directions, projects and opportunities.

Master Plan: N/A

Written Agreements: A standard Letter of Agreement with the Department of Recreation holds the city harmless while Philadelphia Green makes improvements to their property.

Contact:
The Pennsylvania Horticultural Society
Philadelphia Green Program
100 North 20th Street, 5th Floor
Philadelphia, PA 19103
(215) 988-8800

www.libertynet.org/phs

Achieving Great Parks, Conference Proceedings, Project for Public Spaces, 1996.

American Pathways: Case Studies in Successful Partnering for Trails and Greenways, National Park Service, American Hiking Society; 1998.

Beveridge, Charles, and Rocheleau; Frederick Law Olmsted: Designing the American Landscape, Rizzoli, New York, 1995.

Cranz, Galen. The Politics of Park Design. MIT Press, 1982.

Garvin, Alexander, The American City, What Works, What Doesn't, McGraw-Hill, 1995

McPeck, Eleanor M.; Morgan, Keith; and Zaitzevsky, Cynthia, editors; "Olmsted in Massachusetts: the Public Legacy: A Report of the Inventory Committee of the Massachusetts Association for Olmsted Parks," Brookline, Mass, 1983.

Project For Public Spaces, Great Parks/Great Cities, A Leadership Forum, Project For Public Spaces, 1998

Project For Public Spaces, Parks as Community Places, Conference Proceedings, Boston, Project For Public Spaces, 1997.

Project For Public Spaces, Parks as Community Places, Conference Proceedings, San Francisco, CA, Project for Public Spaces, 1998.

Rogers, Elizabeth Barlow, Rebuilding Central Park, a Management and Restoration Plan, MIT Press, 1987.

Schuyler, David and Jane Turner Censer, eds. The Papers of Frederick Law Olmsted, Vol. IV, Johns Hopkins University Press, Baltimore, MD. 1992

Schwartz, Loring LaB., Editor, Charles A. Flink and Robert M. Searns: Greenways, A Guide to Planning, Design and Development Island Press, 1993

Walker, Chris "Partnerships for Parks. Lessons From the Lila Wallace-Reader's Digest Urban Parks Program," The Urban Institute, 1999

How To Turn A Place Around:
A Handbook for Creating Successful Public Places
$30.00

A user-friendly and common sense guide for everyone from community residents to mayors on how to create successful places. The ideas presented in this book reflect Project for Public Spaces twenty-five years of experience in helping people to understand and improve their public spaces. The community-based and "place oriented" process outlined in this book is organized around the eleven basic principles of creating successful public spaces along with methods that anyone can use to evaluate a space

People who read this handbook will learn how to create better public spaces in their own communities and the value of short-term actions and making visible changes. Through examples of people's experiences in other cities, PPS demonstrates that, with an understanding of how a place works, any place can be "turned around."

In a workbook included as an appendix, tools such as observations, surveys, public meetings, are described in a simple, how-to manner that will help citizens get all the information needed to that people can use to understand why some spaces are successful and why some of them are not. It also provides steps that will help one lead a community based visioning process and begin to improve their neighborhood. (2000, Project for Public Spaces, 75 pgs. illustrations)

How Transportation and Community
Partnerships Are Shaping America
Part I: Transit
Part II: Streets and Roads
$5.00 EACH

A series of case studies about transportation partnerships that rely on the input of people who use and experience a place on a regular basis. The studies focus not only upon the bus stop, street or station itself, but also on how these facilities connect to the surrounding districts and public spaces, thus helping to make these areas more economically stable, safe and productive. (Part I: 1999, American Public Transportation Association. 16 pgs, color illustrations; Part II: 2000, American Association of State Highway and Transportation Officials. 26 pgs, color illustrations)

The Role of Transit in Creating Livable
Metropolitan Communities
$30.00

Transit was once an intrinsic part of our communities. Until the late 1950s and early 1960s, trolley lines, train stations, bus stops and other transit facilities provided both connections and friendly settings that knit communities together, spurred economic development and enhanced community life. As the automobile took over, much of this transit presence, along with the synergy it created, disappeared. Now, communities are beginning to realize what they missed, and are building new transit facilities as well as refurbishing long-neglected ones. They're finding that this new infusion of transit can help restore community livability if it is designed and managed in response to local needs. (1997, National Academy Press, Transportation Research Board. 164 pgs, color illustrations.)

Transit-Friendly Streets: Design and Traffic
Management Strategies to support
Livable Communities
$35.00

If designed to accommodate and balance the needs of all users - not just motorists - streets can contribute to the livability of a community by enhancing safety, comfort, and convenience for pedestrians, bicyclists, and transit users alike. For the transit user, better management and design of streets not only can improve reliability of service (by reducing the competition for street space among cars, buses or light rail vehicles), but also can make streets safer and more accessible. The approaches in this book can be combined with other transit strategies to realize even greater social and economic impacts, whether in revitalizing a downtown, restoring cohesiveness to a community, or creating new development opportunities. This study provides examples of cities where the effective, balanced incorporation of transit into city streets is having a positive impact on livability and quality of life. (1998, National Academy Press, Transportation Research Board)

Amenities For Transit Handbook and The Transit Design Game Workbook
$35.00

What do passengers really want when it comes to design features on board buses and at transit stops? What elements affect a person's decision to take transit to work instead of driving? How do passenger preferences differ depending upon their frequency of ridership, length of trip, and sex? Where should transit agencies invest their hard-earned capital funds to get the most ridership "bang for the buck?" Answers to these questions and more can be found in The Amenities For Transit Handbook and The Transit Design Game Workbook. (1999, National Academy Press, Transportation Research Board. 150 pgs, illustrations. Disk included)

Getting Back to Place: Using Streets to Rebuild Communities
$35.00

This publication provides an overview of the vital role streets play in providing a sense of place and a setting where communities can come together; it also reviews the ingredients that can help to make this happen. It includes chapters on traffic calming and other place-making tools, such as developing amenities, activities and management strategies that help build communities; on historical and current successful examples of lively, thriving streets in U.S. and elsewhere; on integrating transit facilities with streets. It also shows how communities can get involved in improvement programs and discusses various approaches to fundraising. Photos from PPS's extensive archive, cartoons, diagrams and drawings provide clear and lively

illustrations of concepts and cases. Pre-publication draft: 78 pgs, illustrations.

Managing Downtown Public Spaces
$21.00

Management is important in making public places lively and usable. In fact, it is often can accomplish more than any urban design scheme. This practical guide shows how to make public places safe, attractive and lively. It focuses on innovative strategies to create a downtown marketplace, supplement city services, improve the design of public places and start a management program. (1984, American Planning Association. 76 pgs, color illustrations.)

Public Markets And Community Revitalization
$27.95

A guidebook covering all aspects of the market development process, from simple, inexpensive farmers and craft markets to large market districts. Shows how public markets can revitalize communities, create opportunities for fledgling entrepreneurs and provide safe and sociable public gathering places. Includes sample budgets, staffing requirements, tenant mix plans, marketing strategies, cash flow analysis and cost projections. Several in-depth case studies and numerous examples of public markets across the United States and Canada are featured. (1995, Project for Public Spaces, Inc. and the Urban Land Institute. 120 pgs, color illustrations.)

To order, contact us at:
Project for Public Spaces
153 Waverly Place, 4th Floor
New York, NY 10014
(212) 620-5660

Or print out and fax an order form from our website at www.pps.org